SWORDS FROM THE NORTH

by the same author

BANG, YOU'RE DEAD!
KILLER IN DARK GLASSES
ASK FOR KING BILLY

Swords from the North

HENRY TREECE

FABER AND FABER
24 Russell Square London

First published in 1967
by Faber and Faber Limited
24 Russell Square, London WC1
Reprinted 1969
Printed in Great Britain
by Latimer Trend & Co Ltd Whitstable

571 08136 3

Contents

Contents

Introduction

This is the story of the famous Norseman, Harald the Stern (Hardrada), between the years 1034 and 1044, which he spent in Constantinople—or Byzantium, or Miklagard—as captain of the Greek Emperor's guard. Harald is of special interest because in 1066 he came to England with three hundred longships in the hope that he would become our king. Instead, beside the river Derwent at Stamfordbridge near York, he was struck dead by an arrow on Wednesday, September 30th. So many of his warriors were slain on this day that only twenty-four longships were needed to take the survivors back home to Norway. In many ways Harald was the last of the great vikings and, though a stern man, was a brave and honest one according to the codes of his time.

The framework on which this story is built is the *Heims Rringla* or Sagas of the Norse Kings, written between 1223 and 1235 by an Icelandic chieftain-poet named Snorri Sturluson, himself a descendant of that Wulf who plays such a large part in this book.

Snorri was not a historian in the sense that we use the word today; he had little access to accurate documents and much of what he says may have come to him by family tradition. However, a saga is first and foremost a story to be enjoyed for its own sake and so, in retelling this one, I have not tried to correct Snorri's history but instead have attempted to interpret and to set down in more modern terms his picture of those heroic and sad times.

Henry Treece

1 · The Chamberlain

The two Icelanders stood back to let Harald go first up the twenty grey stone steps that led from the wharfside to the street.

He had been to great trouble, combing his long yellow hair and his stubbly beard before coming ashore, and now the crowd which lined the railings began to call out in admiration. A dark-skinned girl carrying a basket of green melons on her shoulder cried, "Here comes their king! They must be rich folk in the north. Look at his golden bracelets!"

Everybody sighed or laughed but Hardrada pretended not to see them though his pale blue eyes missed nothing.

Behind him Wulf whispered mockingly, "Go on, Harald, give the poor cattle something to remember. They don't see a viking come ashore every day, I'll be bound."

Haldor slapped the broad iron of his axe and laughed in the bright sunshine. "Perhaps that is just as well," he said.

Now Harald was almost at the top of the stairway and the crowd began to draw back to let this warrior pass.

A light breeze caught his spun-gold hair, flaring it out below the bronze-bound black leather helmet. His long cloak of heavy dark red wool fringed with silver tassels lifted a moment to show the great ivory-hafted longsword in the untanned calf-skin scabbard at his left hip.

The Syrian girl with the melons put her basket down and, with her thin dark hands placed together, rolled up her eyes and sighed, "Oh, to think of such a sweetheart!"

But the men in the crowd did not hear her. They were looking with envy at the Northman's hide shirt, stitched all over with links of dull iron; at the silver-studded belt about his slim waist; at the twisted thongs of deer-hide that bound his blue linen breeks to the shape of his strong legs.

One old man, leaning on a stick, pointed a shaking finger and said, "This is a fighting man, my friends. You don't get a scar like that one, from temple to chin, sitting by the hearth-fire."

For a moment Harald was tempted to tell the old man that this scar had come from nothing more deadly than an apple-bough he had ridden into by night above Trondheim; but just then there was a sudden blare of silver trumpets and along the street clattered a half-squadron of horsemen, riding on either side of a gold-draped litter surmounted by a tall palm tree carved from ebony and bearing leaves of thinly-beaten gold.

"The empress comes!" cried a small boy. "Look, old lady Zoë has come down herself to greet the white wolves!"

Then all at once the three Northmen realized that the crowd had turned away from them as though they were not there, to gaze at the approaching cavalcade.

Only the little melon-seller still sighed, her eyelids closed, her hands clasped tightly in her dream.

Haldor said to Wulf, "So, brother, now you know how much a viking is worth in Miklagard."

Harald stood stern-faced and still. Then he said in a voice like an old iceberg crunching along a rocky headland, "But they will learn, comrades. They will learn. The price is about to go up at any moment now!"

Yet it was not the empress who had come down to the wharf-side after all. The slaves set down the gold-draped litter and out of it stepped a thin-faced bent old man who leaned on an ebony staff. Wulf said with a sigh, "The silver thread the sewing-women used when they embroidered that man's robe would keep a family of five up in Iceland for a year."

Harald slapped him on the back and answered, "Aye, maybe. But if you try to snatch it off his back, brother, you will get stuck so full of lances I shall think we came to Miklagard with a hedgehog as sailing-mate!"

They had no chance to say more, for now the old man was tapping his way towards them, his large dark eyes searching them, weighing them up, as he came; and when he was within three paces of the brothers he said in a high voice, "Which of you is Harald Sigurdson, half-brother to Olaf the Saint?"

Harald moved forward a little way and stroked his golden beard. "I am that one," he said. "Have you come to collect my taxes already? We have only just set foot in your famous city. Come back later in the day to the longship called *Stallion*. By that time we may have had luck betting on one of the horses racing at your Hippodrome."

It was meant to be a joke but the thin old man did not smile, and after he had stared into Harald's face for a long while the viking began to wish he had not spoken. He shuffled his great feet and said lamely, "I spoke in jest, you understand. Now I look more closely I can see that you are not a tax-collector."

That also was a joke of sorts, but the old man's keen stare continued. Then at last he let his thin lips curl into a sort of smile and said bleakly, "I am familiar with Norwegians and their jokes, Sigurdson. We have been entertained by such jokes for ten generations here in Byzantium. I recall that your kinsman Olaf attempted a few of them in his time as captain here. But I am not with you to discuss jokes at this time. I am a Chamberlain of the Court, as you will no doubt come to learn, and my purpose is to take you direct to that Most Serene Majesty, our Empress Zoë."

Wulf blew out his red cheeks and said, "What, to be invited to the palace on our first day! We are in luck, Harald!"

But the Chamberlain did not laugh at this either. He stood

back a little way and bowed his head, indicating the litter with his ebony wand. "Have the goodness to seat yourselves," he said. "The empress has never been kept waiting by anyone and it is unlikely that she will change her habits now because a shipload of Northmen come into harbour looking for easy pickings in the Varangian Guard."

Harald was about to reply to this too, but held his words back at the last moment. Then bending low so as to fit his great bulk into the litter he lay back on the scarlet cushions beside his friends. The Chamberlain entered last and drew the heavy curtains close shut.

Haldor said merrily, "Nay, nay, Chamberlain! We have come far to see Miklagard. Open the curtains, my friend."

The old man leaned on his black stick and clenched his teeth for an instant. Then he said in a voice that might have made many men shiver, "This is the imperial litter, seafarer. Its curtains are never left open. Here we have always acted according to ancient custom according to precedent. Because the Serene Majesty has thought fit to give you an audience it is no reason why she should also change the laws concerning the curtains of her litter. Or are we all wrong in Byzantium, my dear man? Is the empress wrong in keeping her curtains drawn, do you say?"

The three vikings lay back in the heat gazing at him speechlessly. They had not met such a man before though they had been in kings' halls in the north. He was more like a snake than a man, they all thought at the same time. So they said no more but let themselves be jolted along avenue after avenue, alley after alley, until at last they were set down and, when the curtains were drawn open, saw that they were in a great inner square tiled with red and gold and blue. Near to them a fountain made of dull silver threw many jets up into the air. The water came from the open mouths of seven lions whose staring eyes were formed with great rubies.

Harald whispered to Wulf, "Don't say it, or we shall find ourselves in their dungeons before this day is out! Look at the birds and keep your thievish thoughts to yourself."

And truly the birds were worth looking at. They were of a dozen colours, all fluttering and cheeping high in the gilded dome, kept from escaping by a great net hoisted on ebony poles about the square.

Wulf shuddered and said softly, "That is how I feel now, Harald. I would let them shave off my beard even, if only I could be back in *Stallion* along the Dnieper, blow the wind how it might."

Harald only said, "Courage, Icelander, courage! Have we come so far to let an old man with a black stick, and a few poor chirruping birds, put us to fear?"

So they followed the Chamberlain along many dim passages and into the presence of the Empress Zoë.

2 · Empress and Emperor

In the vast dim chamber the air was so heavy, so thick with the scent of incense that the vikings almost sneezed. At first all they could make out was a tall throne of some dark wood, its back carved like the fanning tail of a peacock and its sides rising in the shape of palm trees.

The Chamberlain whispered sternly, "Go forward and kneel."

But Harald said aloud, "What, is this a church? I see no altar."

The Chamberlain struck his wand on the glazed tiles in annoyance, but just then a woman's voice said, "Leave them be, Primikyrios. You know these Northmen, they pray as our forefathers did to Zeus, standing upright."

Harald said, "We are not praying, lady, we are looking round to see what pretty things you have which we might want to take back with us up the river to Kiev."

Even Wulf and Haldor gasped at this, but the woman's voice sounded amused. She said, "Yes, you are of the northern breed, young man. But allow me to tell you that the pretty things in the palace are only distributed when the emperor dies; and even then only to the sworn members of his Varangian Guard."

Harald said lightly, "Then swear us in now, lady, and let us be off."

The black robed Primikyrios snorted with fury behind him at this and even began to raise his wand as though to strike the viking. But the empress came forward from the dusk of the great throne and halted him.

She was more than middle-aged, they saw, and was not the most beautiful woman they had met on their travels. Yet in her flowing robes of pale blue and crimson silk and with her auburn hair piled thickly on her head, she was striking. Harald cast his eye over her and noted the painted eyelids and the long darkened lashes. He noted the gold bracelets that seemed to reach from wrist to elbow, jangling as she moved. But most of all he noted the white watchful face and the cruel bend of the nose. About her floated a musklike perfume which reminded him of some predatory animal, a leopardess, perhaps.

She seemed to flare out her nostrils, gazing directly into his face, then said, "When you address me again, viking, you must call me Your Most Serene Majesty. Do you understand that?"

Harald wiped his broad brown hand across his ruddy face to clear it of moisture in that stifling room. Then he said, "Shall we do as she says, brothers? Or shall we just call her 'lady', as we do our own queens?"

Before the two Icelanders could answer the Empress Zoë cried out sharply, "Primikyrios, draw the curtains to let in more light, then leave us. I have my silver whistle in case I need you again."

And when this was done and the Chamberlain had bowed out backwards from the throne, the empress struck Harald lightly on the cheek with a small ivory spatula that she held in her right hand. Her blow was no more than the fluttering of a butterfly on his bearded face. But he did not like it all the same.

She said smiling, "Nay, do not look like a lion at me, Sigurdson. There are ten thousand men in Byzantium this minute who would count it the greatest honour of their lives to be so struck by me."

Harald said dourly, "In all my life no one has ever struck me unless a second blow followed the first, and that second came from me."

The Empress Zoë sat back on her great throne still smiling. "Then strike me now, viking," she said. "I would not wish to break the pattern of your destiny."

But Harald only fingered the place where her little stick had touched and then said slowly, "That I cannot do, lady, because when I strike the second blow it is the last that is struck, for who receives it needs no other."

She began to laugh so shrilly then that curtains seemed to twitch here and there in the great room, as though men were behind them wondering what was happening and waiting to run in.

Wulf nudged Haldor and whispered, "Be ready. Swing your sword round in your belt so that we can hold them off."

But the empress shook her head and said softly, "Oh, you Northmen! Always suspecting that we of Byzantium are about to ambush you! You are like great children, my friends. Yes, great children."

Then Harald said sternly, "Lady, in the north we learn to be men at an age when the rest of the world are children. If you do not understand us by now that is your misfortune. We come here to sell you the hire of our swords, no more; and after our term with you is done, we shall go back to Norway and sit on our own stools and eat our own food. Nothing more. I bring thirty rovers into haven here, all good men who have stood under the arrows in twelve battles. Will you employ them or not? If your answer is 'No', then we shall sail out again by the late tide and seek another master, in Sicily or Africa, or wherever the sea takes us. It matters little to us as long as the pay is fair. But once we have given our oath we never break our word. We give good value, lady."

The Empress Zoë sucked the end of the ivory spatula and said solemnly, "I'm sure you do, Northman. Yes, I'm sure you do. But, as you see, I am only a weak woman and am not a good bargainer as you fierce men are. Give me until this evening so that I can discuss this matter with my High Constable, the Contostavlos. Now, in the meantime, sit on those cushions that you see before you and tell me something of the north. You know, we in the south, we kings and queens, do not travel much; but we always wish to know what is happening in the world, and sometimes the spies we send out do not report the truth correctly to us."

Harald said, "You should whip them if they do not earn their pay."

The empress glanced away. "We sometimes do worse than that," she said. "But it does not make them better spies, not to have eyes to see with." Then she smiled and looked back at the men. "Tell me your story," she said. "Tell me how you brothers came together, for I can see well enough that you are not true brothers from one mother—but are, as you say, battle-brothers. Tell me."

So Harald told her how he had stood beside his half-brother Olaf at Stiklestad against the Danish invaders, until Olaf fell. He told her he was only fifteen at the time and was glad of the help of Earl Rognvald to get away from the battlefield and to make his way to Novgorod, where his kinsman Jaroslav the Grand Duke sheltered him and betrothed him to his young daughter Elizabeth.

The empress looked amused at this. "Is she a pretty girl?" she asked.

Harald shrugged his bear's shoulders. "She is comely," he said. "I am no great judge of that sort of thing. She will do well enough when the time comes. By then she will learn to keep her tongue reined."

The empress clucked and nodded. "What if you do not go back to Novgorod and claim her?" she asked.

Harald said, "I see no reason why I should not go back. The dowry that goes with her is good. Besides, when the throne of Norway is empty again it is my turn to sit on it. And that I mean to do. Well, a king needs a queen at his side and Elizabeth will make a good queen. Her father is training her well. Yes, I shall go back."

The Empress Zoë fanned herself with a bunch of peacock feathers. She smiled. "Ah, well," she said, "we shall see. We shall see. It could be that a fine young man like you might find a throne and a wife for himself here in the south. Surely that would be the good sort of bargain that you vikings look for?"

Harald said, "I am content with the north, lady. I come here to fill myself a few gold-coffers and to pass a year or two until Norway is ready for me again. I will tell you the rest of my tale."

So he told her how he had made friends with his two battle-brothers, Wulf Ospakson and Haldor Snorreson, both of them down from Iceland looking for gold and adventure when he ran across them.

Zoë said, "Are they trustworthy fellows? I have met Icelanders who are so restless that they can never stay in one place more than a month."

Harald said, "I would trust these two with my helmet War Swine; or my sword Quernbiter; or my mesh shirt Emma; or my ship Stallion. As for staying in one place, only old men stay by the hearthside. Young men must be up and doing."

Then he told her how they had gathered taxes for Jaroslav but had grown so weary of burning down peasant villages, to force the folk to pay, that they had taken ship and had come across the Great Portage and the waterfalls and so down the Dnieper into the Black Sea.

The empress said, "No doubt you had adventures, viking? That part of the world is full of wandering Patzinak horsemen. They do not let the ships come down here without a tussle or two."

Harald said, "We met a few of them but they did not stay long to talk with us when we put ashore and went after them. The thirty rovers in my crew were sad at this; they hoped to learn more of the world from them. Our biggest trouble came from the Bulgars who live on the eastern shores of the Black Sea."

Zoë smiled. "I know where they live, Northman," she said. "We keep a regiment of them here in Byzantium. You will meet some of them before long, if you stay with us."

Harald said, "Why do you employ Bulgars when you have a regiment of Northmen in your Varangian Guard?"

She lowered her painted eyes and said, "The Bulgars keep a close watch on the vikings; and the vikings hold the Bulgars in check. We who govern this Empire cannot afford to let any one body of soldiers have the entire control of our city."

Harald pursed his lips. "Who keeps them both in check then?" he asked. "Do you?"

She smiled and tapped her long thin fingers on the arms of the throne chair. She answered, "My husband Romanus and I are too occupied with more important matters, viking. We employ a general to do that; Georgios Maniakes, a brave soldier who knows how to handle such men as you."

Harald said smiling, "I look forward to meeting him. I am always glad to hear of brave men."

The empress yawned now without holding her jewelled hand over her mouth, so that the vikings should see that their audience was almost ended. She said, "You will meet him. He will send for you to inspect you if the emperor decides that you are men he would care to employ in his Guard."

Harald said, "Let us hope that this Maniakes does not expect us to come running to his whistle. We are not dogs, we are warmen. Where is this emperor, so that we can decide whether we wish to serve him or not?"

The empress was about to answer when one of the curtains was drawn gently aside and a round-shouldered man dressed in a heavy gown of purple silk came shuffling in, leaning hard on a long silver wand. On his bowed head he wore a high crown of chiselled gold, shaped much like the pointed dome of a church. In his left hand he carried a roll of parchment from which a great round seal of red wax dangled.

He stood no higher than Harald's chest but his black eyes were so piercing that the viking almost looked away under their gaze. This old man said dryly, "I am the Emperor Romanus, gentlemen. So, now you have met me, what is your noble decision?"

He stood smiling vaguely, his head nodding all the time under the weight of his tall crown. Harald shrugged his shoulders and said, "Speaking for myself, I have no objection to you, provided the pay is good."

The emperor gave a little smile at this and said, "The pay is good, young man. It is better than any pay in the rest of the world, I might say. I am heartened that you have no objection to me; there are many who have, it seems."

As he said this he turned and glanced at the Empress Zoë, who was gazing at her long tinted fingernails as though she had lost interest in everyone. She did not look back at her husband and so he said, "Then, my good fellows, if you will now kneel and swear on behalf of your ship's crew to serve me faithfully in all that I shall ask until such time as I grant your release, then you shall become members of my Imperial Guard. Is that good enough for you?"

The three men looked at each other. Wulf said outright, "I do not like this kneeling, Harald. We do not kneel in Iceland."

But Harald grinned and said, "Nay, brother, it is nothing. We cannot take an oath looking down on an emperor. So, since he is such a small man, we must kneel. Come, I have no complaint. Do as I do."

So he knelt, in his great bearskin coat with his helmet still on, and his long yellow hair hanging over his broad shoulders. The Icelanders did the same, grumbling, and then, when they had repeated the words of the oath, Romanus struck the three of them on the neck with his silver wand. Then he said, "Now you may rise, Varangers. And if I or my wife or my general command you to swim to Sardinia or fly to the moon, you will do it without question."

Haldor said, "If we can do that, then there must be more magic in that stick of yours than I thought."

The empress laughed with mockery at these words. But Romanus only nodded and said, "It is amazing what magic there is in this staff, Icelander. But this you will come to learn as the years go on."

"Years?" said Harald. "We have only come for months."

The Empress Zoë said from her throne, "There was no mention of months, Varanger. When we employ soldiers, *we* decide how long they shall stay. Now go to the barracks and try on your new armour. General Maniakes will want to see you looking smart for his parade."

The Northmen turned and went towards the curtained door, but they had made no more than three paces when the Empress Zoë clapped her hands so sharply that Harald looked back and said, "Do we walk so well that you must applaud, lady?"

The empress narrowed her eyes and answered, "Quite the contrary, Varanger. You walk so badly that, but for your Norse ignorance, it would be my duty to have you all thrashed against stakes before the people in the Hippodrome tomorrow."

The emperor clucked and nodded so excitedly that his tall heavy crown slipped forward and almost came off. Harald said, "I have never been thrashed in my life and I do not mean to start now."

He began to go back towards the high throne, but Wulf and Haldor had seen the curtains across all the alcoves moving and they took his arms and held him. Then Zoë said, "Your two dogs are wiser than their master, it seems. Perhaps they will understand when I tell them that all our servants of whatever rank, from the Logothete of the Dome to the Curopalates, must move from the presence of the Basileus and myself backwards and bowing. Now let us see if you have learned your first lesson."

The three Northmen backed from the room, red-faced and furious. As they passed through the curtain they heard Zoë's mocking laughter and the emperor's high bleating cackle.

Harald Hardrada said, "By the loaves and fishes, I am inclined to go back in there and teach them both a lesson of my own, these painted puppets!"

But just then a small voice behind them said, "That is what they expect of you, sir. But if you do, you will be dead before I could say even one small prayer for you."

3 · Maria and Theodora

The three northern brothers swung round and there, in the dim and curtain-hung corridor, they saw a thin pale-faced girl of about twelve, dressed in coarse black robes and holding a large silver crucifix against her chest with crossed white hands.

Her dark eyes were so large and sad that Wulf said, "Now, now, little one, there is no need for tears. No one is dead yet. Tell us, who are you to be so concerned about three rough outlanders?"

She lowered her large eyes and said, "I am Maria Anastasia Argyra, Varanger."

Harald held out his hand towards her and said, smiling now, "Then, Maria Anastasia Argyra, take hold of my hands and I will swing you up on to my back and give you the best ride you've ever had down these musty old corridors."

But the girl shrank away from him and shook her head. "Please don't touch me, sir," she said. "I am niece to the Empress Zoë. I am a princess and must not be touched."

Harald rubbed his yellow beard in amusement. "You seem like a small girl to me," he said. "Besides, in my own land there are many who think of me as a king. Cannot a king play with a princess?"

Maria shook her head again. "Here things are different," she said, quite sternly now. "We stand at the centre of the world, in the Holiest of Empires. You, though I can see you are a strong and handsome man, are only a barbarian from the north who chooses to call himself a king. Please follow me and do not try to touch me again for there are eyes watching everywhere in this palace."

She turned and went quickly along the corridor. The Northmen shrugged their shoulders and followed. Here and there, at cross-roads in the many passageways, court servants, in dark robes and bearing black wands, bowed their heads to the little girl, though she paid no attention to any of them.

Harald said to her, "Well, I can see now that you are a princess. And where is Your Highness taking us? To the barracks?"

Maria said over her shoulder, "Do not call me Highness. I am in disgrace and am not allowed a title until I am obedient again. My other aunt, Theodora, to whom I am taking you, wishes me to enter a convent. So I am in disgrace for refusing. Please walk a little faster, Varangers, or I shall be in more trouble for being so long away."

They did as she asked and soon she led them down a low tunnel and into a room so bare that it seemed like a prison to them. In the middle of the grey stone floor kneeled a white-haired old lady dressed in brown sackcloth, wearing a length of thick knotted rope about her neck. As they entered, she gazed at them with faded eyes and said in a surprisingly strong harsh voice, "It is my custom to meet all who enter our service, Varangers. Are you Christians?"

Harald said, "We were baptized at Trondheim. Is that good enough?"

The lady Theodora answered flatly, "It will have to do, meagre as it is. Now kneel before me while I finish my prayers. And you too, girl, kneel behind them and keep your mind on your devotions. Hurry now."

The old lady was a long time in finishing her prayers. She mumbled on in a language that the Northmen could not follow, and every time they thought she had come to the end and were about to rise she began again and again, until their very knee-bones were sore.

But at last she was silent, and when they saw her get up

slowly and stiffly, they rose too and stood before the little plain oak stool where she now sat. And when she had gazed at each one of them, from head to foot, she said, "You have come to Byzantium for easy pickings, like all Northmen. But you will find soon enough that you have wandered stupidly into a spider's web. Last month four English Varangers lost their tongues in the Hippodrome for forgetting how to address the Logothete of the Secretes."

Haldor said, "Trust the English to forget! They would forget their heads if they were loose!"

Theodora said drily, "Some of them have done that, too, Outlander. But usually the eyes are what are forgotten. We are an old people and hence a humane one; but we must force ourselves to treat barbarians with barbarism when their uncouth behaviour deserves it. If you can only learn that you will be wise. Learn also that my niece, Maria Anastasia Argyra, is a silly child who must not be encouraged in her girlish foolishness. Soon she is to enter one of our imperial convents for the good of her wayward soul—I have not decided which one yet—so I forbid you to turn the child's head with any of your godless northern stories. I, the Mother of the People, forbid it. Do you understand?"

Harald glanced over at the kneeling girl Maria and winked at her. She turned her head away like a frightened bird. He said to the old lady then, "You are addressing a man whose half-brother is a saint. Is it likely, do you think, that my stories would be godless ones?"

He felt pleased with himself that he had avoided giving this fierce old crone a promise. But she smiled up at him with her thin white lips and said, "You are as crafty as the rest of Northmen, Varanger, but do not let your pride cost you too dearly."

Suddenly she bent and rang a small silver handbell that stood on the stone floor beside her stool. A panel in the wall behind her slid open and a man came in.

He was not so tall as Harald, but every inch as broad in the shoulder. His face was pale and set in a brooding expression. His eyebrows and hair were jet black. Over his embossed gilt armour he wore a scarlet cloak edged with purple. Under his arm he carried a silver helmet crested with white horse-hair. Before him, crossed one over the other, hung two swords in blue scabbards, a short stabbing *gladius* and a longer *spatha,* after the ancient Roman style.

Theodora said in a thin voice, "This is your master now, Outlanders. This is your general, my kinsman, Georgios Maniakes. Listen to his commands and obey him like slaves in all things."

Harald Hardrada stared at the general coldly, hoping to beat down the Greek's dark gaze. But Maniakes looked back so fixedly that for an instant Harald feared that his own eyes might give way.

Then all at once the general said in a deep voice, "How many battles have you three been in?"

Harald tried to remember, for there had been many against the Danes and the Bonders and the Wends, and some of them little more than ambushes.

He said at last, "I would say twelve, give or take one or two. A fighting man does not count such things as carefully as he would his pay."

Georgios Maniakes smiled scornfully and said, "It will be a month before you count that. We must see what you are worth first. Now tell me, how many times in your twelve great battles did you run away?"

Harald gritted his teeth until Wulf thought he would break them off. He said, "If you are trying to taunt me, wait until we are somewhere outside, with room to move in, Greek."

The general coldly ignored these words and said, "Between you, how many men have you killed?"

Now Haldor spoke up and said, "In the place where I come

from we are taught that it ill becomes any man to boast over the luck which sat on the point of his sword. It may be well enough down in Miklagard for young cocks to crow in the sunlight but up in Iceland the eagle goes quietly about his trade."

Then the General Maniakes turned to Theodora and said, "Gracious One, I think that these three will do. They are much like all the other good ones we have had. It must be the climate they endure up there in the north that makes them so hardy."

He bowed and went back through the sliding panel. And Theodora smiled at Harald and said, "Go now, and see that your weapons are burnished and in good order. The general will not always be so gentle with you."

When they were outside in the corridor again Wulf said to his friends, "I may be wrong, brothers, but I think that this general may give us some trouble before we leave Miklagard."

Haldor answered, "It would suit me better to be up the Dnieper now with the planks bucking under my feet and the wind in my nostrils."

But Harald slapped them both on the shoulder and laughed. "Why," he said, "when have I known you two upset by a musty old palace and a little man in gold armour? Come, come, my lads, let us enjoy our holiday!"

They went off laughing then and all the black-robed chamberlains leaning on their wands stared after them in shocked amazement.

4 · The Varangers

The northern brothers and their crew found the lodgings at the imperial barracks comfortable enough, once they had convinced the other five hundred Varangers that they would not be meddled with. An Orkneyman named Eystein Baardson, shipmaster of the *War Hawk*, came with his crew to their help on the first night. Years before this Eystein had borrowed a cloak and a pair of shoes from Olaf, Harald's half-brother, but had been unable to pay back the debt before his friend was killed at Stiklestad. So now he came to Harald's aid and considered that this was fair return for the cloak and shoes. He saw to it that the newcomers had broad beds close to the windows, and a place at the feast-board within five paces of the kitchen hatchway. More, he said, he could not do.

He told Harald that the Englishmen among the Varangers were quiet enough men unless they got drunk on their own special feast days; but that the Danes and the Normans were hardly ever to be trusted. Harald said, "I have met them before in other places. They are men like any others. Treat them well and they are good enough. Why, I have friends among the yellow-faced Patzinaks whose language I cannot even speak. But I am glad to hear your opinion of these English, for one of these days, when I grow to my full strength, I mean to visit their land and to see if they have a crown there that would fit me."

Eystein Baardson laughed at this and said, "Let me know when you go there for I always fancied being an earl in England."

Harald nodded and said, "I give you my word that when I am king in England, you shall be an earl. And my brothers, Haldor Snorreson and Wulf Ospakson, shall be two of the other earls. We will take some new blood into that country, for I think it is getting to be a very tired old place."

Then a man with a chest like a barrel and a black shade over his left eye stood up from the bench and struck Harald in the middle of the chest with the flat of his hand, almost staggering him, and said, "My name is Gyric and I come from a place you have never heard of called Lichfield in Mercia."

Harald looked down at the man's big red hand and said, "At first I thought it was Thor come visiting from Valhalla. Well, Gyric of Lichfield, I have seen bigger men than you, but not many. What is it you wish to tell me?"

The man said, "I wish to tell you that I am an Englishman and that before you sit on the throne in England you will need to grow to seven feet."

Harald Sigurdson said pleasantly, "I am well on the way to that now, Englishman. But I will bear in mind what you advise me and I will wait until I am the proper height."

Then he turned to the table with Eystein Baardson for the servants had just run in with great wooden troughs full of hot sausages and barley bread. But the Englishman took him by the shoulder and swung him round again. He said, "With this hand I once felled Earl Godwin, and what I could do to him I could do to you. Before I came to Micklagard I was a blacksmith and in my time I shod many war horses and they stood still while I did it."

Wulf and Haldor came closer but Harald waved them back and said gently, "Gyric of Lichfield, I have felt the weight of your hand and I can believe that you were indeed a blacksmith. But be a good lad now and go back to your ale-cup, for I can see that you are about to meddle in something that is not learned at the anvil."

He smiled in the most friendly fashion as he spoke and did not loose his thumbs from his belt once. Then Gyric of Lichfield suddenly struck out at him with clenched fist, but Harald moved a little to the right and slid the blow off his shoulder. Then with the edge of his open hand he struck the Englishman twice on the neck and stepped back so that he could fall without hindrance.

And when Gyric was able to sit up again and was shaking some sense back into his head, Harald Sigurdson bent over him and said. "That is a blow we call Thor's Kiss. It is useful when a man has left his axe at home. One day when you have the time I will teach you how it is done for I can tell that you are the sort of man who might need to know such a trick."

Three men lifted Gyric to his feet but he still could not stand without help, so they put him on the bench near to the sausage troughs where he had only to reach out a little way to help himself. Then Gyric said to Harald, "Norseman, you are a better man than Earl Godwin ever was. When you go to England for the crown I would like to ride with you if you will have me."

Harald Sigurdson picked up a dark blood-sausage and stuffed it into the man's mouth to silence him. Then he said, "That you shall, Gyric of Mercia, but I cannot promise too many earldoms yet awhile. Maybe you will have to be contented with a blacksmith's shop in Lichfield, if that will do."

From that moment Harald had no closer friend in Micklagard than the Englishman, who was famous among all the taverns and gaming-houses in the city as a fierce man to face. And because Gyric was Harald's friend now, all the other English Varangers swore to stand by the Norseman too. Indeed, if he had known it at that time, with those two blows on the blacksmith's neck he had gained himself an army.

5 · The Axe Game

But not all meetings were so fortunate. Every morning the Varangers were required to escort the emperor to Hagia Sophia, past aqueducts and cisterns and along vast colonnades of white marble. There it was his custom to deliver a sermon or to read from some theological work and then, as he left, to offer to the Patriarch a bag of gold in token of which the tall crown of the Basileus was returned to him.

Then, on most afternoons when the sun was blazing down outside, it was his habit to sit on his enormous throne that was decorated with gold plane and pomegranate trees on the boughs of which gold birds sat and sang by clockwork. This was usually done to impress visiting envoys from Germany, or Persia, or even India; and at a certain secret signal from the emperor this throne was raised by water-pressure in hidden ducts so that it seemed to float in the air high above the heads of the kneeling visitors, who were always amazed or pretended to be so.

After the new Varangers had seen this happen a dozen times, and had become weary of the foolish performance, they would spend the time between morning and afternoon duties in an open space behind the Hippodrome where there were set a hundred thick ash stakes to which wild beasts were often tethered before one of the bigger shows. And here the northern Varangers invented their own axe game on which they gambled to pass the hours away. One man would wet his forefinger and mark a point on a stake, then stand away; his opponent would sight that mark, take his stance, close his eyes and sweep out with the two-handed axe that they all carried. If it was a good blow, then the stake fell, shorn off at the exact mark, and the axe-man won his bet. But if it was a poor stroke then the axe bit only half-way through, or missed the mark entirely.

One hot afternoon while the emperor was being hoisted in his throne to impress an ambassador from Bagdad, Harald was sitting in the dust of the Hippodrome corral watching his crewmen playing the axe game and cheering or laughing at what he saw, when suddenly from behind him he saw a sharp black shadow cast upon the dry ground and heard a high voice shout out, "Stand to your feet, you Norse scum, when your captain deigns to come among you."

Harald turned his head and saw that the general, Georgios Maniakes, was standing five paces away from him, his helmet crest fluttering in the light breeze, his scarlet cloak whipping out behind him, and his pale face lined with fury.

All the Varangers looked towards Harald, who said quietly, "General, we are doing what we are paid for—practising with our weapons to guard the emperor."

Maniakes' dark eyes flashed. He said, "You are paid to be at hand where the Basileus Rhomaion himself is. You are not paid to sit in the dust amusing yourselves while His Most Serene Majesty might at this very moment be falling under the knife of a murderer."

Harald yawned in the sunshine and then said slowly, "If such a thing happened, it would not speak well for the emperor's general, whose place it is to be at his post, watching that magic chair jigging up and down."

The new Varangers began to laugh at this but those who had seen some service quietened them abruptly. Georgios Maniakes shuddered inside his gilt armour at the laughter; the sweat sprang from his pale face in little pearls and ran down to his oiled beard. He was a man about to fall dead with some terrible sudden emotion.

Then all at once his black shadow flashed over the grey dust towards Harald, moving like an arrow or a pent-up spring, and the Northmen saw with horror that he held a sword in each hand. At the same time they heard his hoarse scream of fury.

Harald did not rise or draw his own sword. Instead he moved again to his right and swept out his left leg like a great scythe in the corn. Where his head had been, the two swords of Maniakes still shuddered, deeply embedded in the ash stake against which Harald had been leaning. And the general was rolling in the dust, his helmet spinning from him, his scarlet cloak wrapped about his body, holding his arms like a pinion.

The silence over the Hippodrome lay heavy now, and all the Northmen stood still as though they waited for the gods' thunder to roar out.

Then General Maniakes got to his feet and picked up his helmet with its dirtied plume. He did not speak for the tears streamed down his white face and he could not trust his voice to obey him. Instead, he held up his right hand in a signal and a score of Bulgars ran forward, their lances at the ready. They ringed Harald as though he was a dangerous beast, pushing their spear-points into his face. He looked up at them for a while, then said, "There are some who would say that you Bulgars are a cautious folk. How many of you does it take to catch a rabbit?"

Then they took his sword and axe from him and hauled him to his feet. Wulf and Haldor began to run forward but Eystein and Gyric dragged them back.

The Bulgars pushed Harald before them with their lances while another Company ran from cover and prodded back the Northmen. One of the Bulgar lieutenants shouted out, "If you stir to help this wild boar his eyes will be put out. It is as simple as that. He will be blind."

Eystein whispered grimly, "That is likely to happen to him in any case, at having humbled this Maniakes so."

They drove Harald on until they came to an alley that led from the Forum of Constantine. Here there was a row of stone pens, thick-doored and windowless, into which fierce cattle were put to await the butcher. Into the lowest and darkest of these pens they drove Harald, pushing their iron at him savagely.

Before they closed the door on him and shut all sunlight out, he turned and called, "Where is the little soldier Maniakes? Tell him to brush his cloak down before he goes on parade tomorrow. It ill becomes a general to look so sorry for himself."

One of the Bulgars drove his lance butt on to Harald's neck and he fell forward into the darkness.

6 · Harald's Song

It was not the best night that Harald had ever spent. The air of the cell was thick and foul and there was a fly buzzing about in the darkness. Worst of all the place was so small that he had to lie hunched up, unable to stretch his very long legs.

He rubbed the back of his neck from time to time and wished he had had a chance to see which Bulgar had struck him from behind. Then the thought came to him that he might never see anyone again. He had often heard, in his weeks at Micklagard, of this blinding of theirs. It was usually done in the Hippodrome before great crowds with a white-hot iron held very close to the eyes but not touching them, for it was a part of the Greek belief that a man must be whole in body if he is to rise again at the Day of Judgement.

Harald thought for a while what strange folk these Byzantines were. They seemed to live in a little smothered world of their own—and yet they all thought they were so very important and that their way of doing things was the only right way. He wondered how many Greeks there were. There couldn't be many, or they wouldn't make up their army from the men of Italy and France and England and Denmark and Norway and Sweden—and even Turkland.

His mind strayed to the various places he had visited. He pictured King Jaroslav and young Elizabeth with her golden hair and the talking-bird on her finger. Then he pictured Wulf and Haldor and even his new friends Eystein and Gyric. Then his thoughts darted back to his great half-brother Olaf who had looked after him so gently until that terrible battle at Stiklestad. And suddenly Olaf seemed to be in that stifling cell with him, filling the place with bright light and saying, "Why are you moping about things, little brother? You never used to mope when we were together. Pluck up your courage, Harald, for things are never as bad as they seem. You were always a brisk lad at making rhymes and songs, set your mind at making a song now. It will help to pass the time away."

Then the brightness faded in the cell and Olaf was gone.

Harald rubbed his eyes and said, "Aye, that I will, brother. Thank you for reminding me." And so he set about making a song. It was not the best song he had ever made but it served its purpose. And this is what it was:

The black bears dance in Novgorod
And cocks crow in Kiev,
While I lie starved in Micklagard
Waiting for my death.

The moon shines bright on Marmara,
The stars glint on the Dome;
Ere glows the dawn down the Golden Horn
I'll be sailing home.

It's a clear run up the Bosphorus,
Clearer through the Black Sea;
But set me on the Dnieper—
That's the run for me!

Set me on the Dnieper
With tall prow pointing north,
And I vow I'll never come meddling again
To this part of the earth!

He tried this song over a few times and thought that the rhymes could have been better. He knew a scald named Stuv up near Bergen who would have helped him with those rhymes for the price of a horn of barley beer, and have been glad to. But Bergen was a long way off and perhaps old Stuv was dead now. It was a sad thought to think of scalds dying. It was not so bad with warriors, because in their trade they had to go sooner or later. But poets and singers ought to last for ever. Then again it was just as sad to think of good horses going or of good swords wearing out or getting broken. It was worse to think of good ships getting stove in and foundering in lonely places, up distant fiords, or on sea-swept skerries away beyond Orkney with only the gulls left to mourn them and the green weed growing over them at last. It was even worse on the Greenland run. It was so lonely.

Harald felt the tears starting to come out of his eyes at the thought of wrecked ships, so he stopped thinking about them and tried to make a little tune that he could sing his song to. This was even harder than making the words. He wanted it to be a merry tune, but the only things he could think were mournful sounds like those that seals make off rocky coasts at night, or that gannets make before they fall from high rock columns, or that cormorants make when there seems to be no fish for supper.

Harald was telling himself that he was not the best scald in the north, even for a king, when the door of the little cell was flung open violently and a voice shouted out, "Come forth, Hardrada! Come forth!"

Harald thought: Well, at least this puts an end to all this worrying about rhymes and tunes.

So he turned round and crawled forwards out of the cell, his eyes blinded by the bright morning sun. He saw men's feet all about him at last and thought: Well, it ill becomes a man to die on his hands and knees. I had better try getting up.

And this he did. Then he saw that Wulf and Haldor were there laughing with Eystein and Gyric beside them. And all along the alley, stretching thickly as far as the Forum of Constantine, stood the Varangers with their axes in their hands, all laughing and cheering. Some of them were English, some Danes, some Franks, and some even Italians.

Wulf said proudly, "You see, brother, we have come for you."

Harald nodded. He said, "You might have come earlier, then my legs wouldn't be so stiff." He made his voice as gruff as he could.

Eystein said, "Why should you worry about your stiff legs when you have five hundred men to carry you?"

Then his four close friends hoisted him up on to their shoulders and carried him into the Forum with all the Varangers crowding round and shouting as though it was a feast day. And as they went towards the great mass of the imperial palace people in the streets joined the crowd and sang their own sorts of songs. Some of them, the girls mostly, even began to fling red flowers towards Harald. But the Varangers told them to be off about their kitchen duties and not to meddle in men's affairs.

And when they reached the main gates of the palace the Bulgar Guard lowered their spear-points and let them pass through.

Harald said, "There has been a sudden change. Maniakes will not like this."

Wulf said, "Then he can lump it. He is in disgrace with Zoë for taunting you. They say she even threatened to have him whipped in public. These Greek whippings are no joke, it seems."

Harald said, "Nay, nay, that is no proper way to treat a soldier. He was only doing his duty. After all I taunted him as much as he taunted me, so that's fair. I bear him no grudge."

Haldor said, "Then tell Zoë that, for she has sent for you. Now let us wash your face and comb your hair and beard before you go before her."

But Harald said, "That I'll not allow. I'll stand before her as I am or not at all."

So they had to give in and let him stride into her chamber just as he was, with his hair all tangled and his beard matted and the dust upon his arms and legs.

7 · The New Emperor

He stood in the doorway like a shaggy northern god with the pale amber sun behind him and the great sword swinging at his side. The Empress Zoë came forward out of the dimness of the chamber with her hands outstretched. He noticed that she had on three more bracelets than when he last saw her and all were of heavy dull gold. He thought: These would buy a longship in Hedeby, and two longships in Dublin where the men work for a lower wage.

He said, "It is a fine morning, Zoë."

She stiffened and answered, "I sent for you, Varanger."

He walked past her into the chamber and sat down on her throne chair. Then after a while he said, "I should have come whether or not. When a king-to-be is thrown into gaol like a common pick-purse he expects to discuss it, even if it is only with a woman."

For a long time the Empress of the Whole World struggled to keep her temper in. At last she said calmly, "You are sitting in my chair, Varanger."

Harald looked down as though he noticed it for the first

time. Then he said smiling, "It is a mighty uncomfortable chair, to tell the truth. For all its pretty carvings it is harder than many a cowherd's stool I have sat on up in Snowland." Then he got up and gave the chair a kick to show her what he thought of it and of Micklagard.

She sat down then and regarded him with fixed wide-open eyes. "You are a man," she said at last. "You are a fool also; but first of all you are a man. There are not too many men in the world. So I sent for your release from the slaughter-pen."

Harald turned his back on her and walked towards the nearest alcove. Bending suddenly he twitched the heavy curtain open. No one was there.

He turned and smiled. "This is different from last time, woman," he said.

She bowed her head and answered, "Yes, it is different, Varanger. For now I trust you. Indeed I have to trust you since I have offended General Maniakes on your behalf."

Harald began to laugh. "Come, come, woman," he said, "Maniakes and Harald Sigurdson—they are not the only two men in Byzantium. You have your emperor to trust still. That little man with the gold tower on his bent head. You have him, Romanus."

The empress rose slowly from her chair and said gravely, "Romanus is dead, Harald."

Harald looked at her in wonder. "I escorted him yesterday to Hagia Sophia," he said. "He was in great spirits and laughing all the way at some joke or another he made to his Chamberlain."

Zoë answered, "He was not laughing when I saw him last, in the small hours of this morning while you lay in the pen. No, he was doing everything, but not laughing."

Harald came closer to her and said sternly, "And what else was he doing, woman?"

She lowered her eyes and said, "He was doing what men do

when they have drunk poison, captain. He was crying out and praying and making horrible sounds besides."

Harald said, "It is not a death I know much about. He must have sorely wished to be rid of his life to take poison. Why do you call me captain, woman?"

The Empress Zoë stood to her full height and said, "Because that is what you are now, viking. All the Varangers met in the night and elected you as their captain. They threatened me that if you were not set free and made captain, then they would burn the imperial palace and all in it."

Harald laughed and said, "Ah, they are great jesters, these north folk. You should not take them seriously. They will say anything for a joke, woman."

Zoë frowned and answered, "It is a stark jest when they bring the torches into the state rooms, viking. It is rather more than a jest when they tip over five marble fountains and pick the ruby eyes out of the carved lions with their dagger-points."

Harald nodded. "Aye," he said, "they carry it a bit too far at times, I know. But I must say, I thought of taking those rubies myself."

"Too far," she echoed. "If I did not wish to marry you, I should have had them all hanged for mutiny, and you blinded for inciting it."

Now it was Harald's turn to frown. He said, "I do not hear very well first thing in the morning. It is something to do with a blow I took on the head outside Kiev, collecting taxes."

Zoë came forward again and said stiffly, "Then I will help your deafness, Harald, and I will repeat—Byzantium has lost its emperor. Byzantium, which is the centre of the whole world and of Christendom, urgently needs a strong man to guard it. Who better than Harald Sigurdson, a great captain and a man of royal blood? I ask again, will you marry me and become the first man in all the world?"

Now Harald suddenly sat on the mosaic floor and began to laugh so loudly that Wulf and Haldor ran in with their swords out, thinking he was in pain. He saw them and said, pointing at the empress, "Do you know what she has just asked me?"

But before he could tell them he had gone off into a fit of laughter again.

Wulf said, "He is suffering from his night in the bullock-pen. It was enough to turn any man's head. Come on, up you get, brother, and we'll put some good food into you."

Haldor turned to ask permission of the empress to carry the captain through the private passageway to the barracks, but she had already run out, ashamed at Harald's laughter.

The next day just at dawn forty heralds went through the city announcing to all the people that their Serene Majesty Zoë had consented to marry Michael Catalactus of Paphlagonia and to elevate him to the state of emperor.

Two days after that the same heralds went out again and this time proclaimed that it was the wish of the new emperor that his armies under the joint command of Georgios Maniakes and Harald Sigurdson should sail down through the Aegean Islands to show all the world the new might that had come to Byzantium.

When Harald heard this news he was on his way to draw pay for all his men from the Grand Domestic in the Paymaster's office of the palace. He halted and smiled at the herald who told him, then, turning suddenly, caught sight of a little dark-robed figure he knew, peering at him with wide eyes from behind a curtain. Quickly he bent forward and switched the curtain away and there stood the Lady Maria Anastasia Argyra.

"Well, well, sweetheart!" he shouted in high glee. "So you have heard the good news? We are off to smell the sea again and maybe to fight a few good battles instead of kicking our heels in this smelly old city."

The Lady Maria began to weep then and to mumble that battles were terrible and most unChristian. Harald bent before her and dried her eyes on the bright scarlet sleeve of his new captain's tunic. Then he said suddenly, "Hey, it was wrong for a rough Outlander to touch a princess, remember? But for an equal of the great General Maniakes, what? For the one and only Captain of Varangers, what?"

She smiled up at him now, so he swung her on to his shoulders and galloped off down the dim corridors, neighing like a war horse, with the princess laughing louder than she had ever done in her life before.

When word of this was taken to Theodora in her grey cell, she drew her white lips together and said, "So, it is as I thought. The viking has set himself out to make the child a bigger fool than she already was. Well, there is nothing we can do about it at the moment; but as soon as the ships sail out there shall be a reckoning. I will make that silly little girl sorry that she ever lowered herself to talk to a Norseman."

All the ladies in waiting bowed at this and the Chamberlains with their black wands shook their heads as though Harald had indeed brought devil's disaster and the wrath of God upon their eternal city.

8 · Council Chamber

The new emperor Michael Catalactus was in most ways different from Romanus. His family had come from the southern shores of the Black Sea and he himself looked more like a Syrian of the deserts than a Greek. His skin was dark and his body wiry but strong. Although he was still in his prime the hair at his temples and above his ears had turned to white. The deep lines that reached from his nostrils down either side of his thin mouth gave him a sombre, even cruel look. He spoke Greek with a strong Armenian accent which caused certain of the palace Council to shake their heads as though a barbarian had been allowed into their midst. One of the first things he did was to have the high crown of Basileus, last worn by Romanus, melted down and remoulded into another shape to fit his own head. The new design was drawn by a travelling artist from Tiflis and conveyed the shape of an eagle crouching with wings held down, over the carcass of a lion. Neither the artist nor the emperor could say what this design meant; but with the wings on either side of his fine head and the lion's tail jutting as stiffly behind him as the predatory beak jutted before, he looked a splendid sight as he strode, two days after Good Friday, to his wedding with the ageing empress.

This was the last state occasion in which Harald's Varangers took a part before they set out for the distant islands; so they put on a very good show and avoided becoming drunk until the sun had set. This was difficult for them since the Bulgar Regiment had started to celebrate the wedding almost from early morning.

Eystein came to Harald in the Mess at noon and said, "If we had any scores to settle with those black-faced apes now would be the time. They are lying in every street and corner, unable to lift a finger, let alone a lance."

And Harald gazed at him sternly and said, "Eystein, dear comrade, I can well understand your opinion. And do not think that I am ungrateful. But when the day comes that I choose to settle scores with these Bulgars, I shall see to it that they are sober and in their right minds and that they outnumber the Northmen by three to one. Only in that way do I settle my scores."

Then Eystein Baardson fell to his knees and put his forehead on his captain's shoe and said, "I am ashamed, Harald. If I ever speak so again I beg that you will point out my stupidity to me as you did to Gyric of Lichfield."

Harald Sigurdson raised him up and said merrily, "Old Eystein, together, you and I will see many things in this world. But one thing we shall never see is the breaking of our great friendship. Now go and tell the Varangers of the third company to set their helmets on straight this afternoon. They are all Danes and like to look a little different from the Englishmen, and so they will wear their gear at the back of their fat heads. I do not dare tell them myself or they might knock me down. But you can do it for me."

Eystein clenched his jaws and said, "If any Dane questions your order I will see that there is one Dane less in the world inside a breathing-space."

Harald called after him, "Do not be too rough with them. They are good enough fellows, though a little stubborn."

That evening when the city was quietening, Michael Catalactus sent for Harald Sigurdson, into an inner room which had no windows. He was sitting at a silver table inlaid with amethysts and jade but had taken off his heavy robes and sat among his papers dressed only in a thin white linen shirt. He had even laid his new crown aside.

And when the Varanger captain strode in, the emperor smiled and said, "Do not bow, Harald; and excuse me if I do not rise to greet you. Today has been a great trial to me with all that parading and speech-making and ceremonial. I intend to cut it down if I am allowed to be emperor for long. It grows tedious and it makes our people the laughing-stock of the world. What do you think?"

Harald was just about to tell him what he honestly thought when he saw in the emperor's eyes a curious amber glint that reminded him of a wolf he had watched once, waiting for its prey above a sheep-pen in Kurland. So he drew back his words, bowed his head gently and said, "Each people has the right to its own customs, Majesty. I know more about axe-play than ceremonial, so who am I to advise such as you?"

Michael Catalactus smiled wryly, then with his own hand poured out a glass of wine for Harald; but the Norseman shook his head and said, "Majesty, I should die of shame to set my lips to the cup before you. I beg you do not dishonour me but drink first."

He held out the cup to the emperor, who looked startled for a moment, then shook his head and said, "You are wise, Hardrada. Why do we need to drink, and of such a poor thin vintage, we who are sworn friends? See, I will cast this miserable wine away."

Harald moved his feet secretly so that the wine should not splash over his legs and feet.

Then suddenly that wolf look came back into Michael's eyes and he said, "Hardrada, as one man to another, if in the future you hear the rumour that I gave poison to old Romanus to drink, what will you think of me?"

Harald looked him straight in the eye and said, "I shall think that I would trust you exactly as much as I have trusted you before. Such rumours would make no difference to what I think of my emperor."

Then Michael Catalactus rose and said, "That is all I wished to be sure of, captain. I can see that my Varangers have a worthy leader in all their strategy. Now good night and may you sleep well before your long voyage."

As Harald bowed from the room he saw that where the wine had fallen on to parchments on the tiled floor, the thin sheepskin had gone shrivelled and brown.

He said, "Good night, my lord. And may you sleep as soundly as I intend to do."

He shut the door on that wolf look again, then turned sharply in time to swing sideways as the Bulgar guard struck out at him with a curved sword. The blade passed over his head and Harald took the man by the neck of his mesh shirt and flung him hard against the stone wall. He fell senseless to the floor. Then Harald picked up that man's sword and bent it over his knee until it looked like a horse-shoe. This he wound round the man's neck as a collar that he would find when he woke much later.

So Harald went back to the barracks and joined his men.

9 · The Gold Chain

Wulf and Haldor were awake and sitting on their pallets, staring moodily at their weapons hanging on the wall beside them. When they saw Harald they jumped up and greeted him with relief.

Wulf said, "We are glad to see you back here in one piece. It is our opinion that you should not trust that man, the emperor."

Harald drew off his mail coat and lay upon his bed laughing. "You are like two hens clucking at my heels," he said. "Do you think I am your chicken? As for the emperor, he seems a quiet enough little man to me. You must learn to be more charitable in your judgement, brothers."

Then he rolled over with his face to the wall and went to sleep.

Now the next morning, when the Varangers were making ready to go down to the galleys at Contoscalium Port, the High Chamberlain accompanied by a Protostrator carrying a box of black ebony entered the barracks and bowed before Hardrada. He was struggling to lace on a thigh-piece and so paid small attention to them, only nodding in a friendly way.

The High Chamberlain said gravely, "We come from the Emperor of the World, who regrets that you were waylaid last night and has since had the Bulgar ruffian punished as he deserves."

Harald paused in his lacing and said, "That is a shame, for now the poor fellow has suffered twice for one mistake. No man, even a Bulgar, should be expected to pay double. Anyway, I hope he is well now."

The Protostrator, aware of his importance as an imperial messenger, said drily, "He is as well as can be expected. By the Grace of God he may walk again in a few weeks." Then in a more official tone he said, "I am here from the Most Serene Majesty to give you this box in which you will find a token of his esteem for you."

Wulf stepped forward and said, "Don't open it, brother. There may be a snake in it that will bring your death on you."

But Harald smiled at him and flicked open the lid with his great thumb. Inside on a bed of gleaming crimson silk lay a broad gold chain, each section of which was inlaid with precious stones in blue and red and green. At the end of this chain hung an enormous medallion showing the head of Michael Catalactus wearing his new crown.

Harald nodded his head gently and said, "I have seen worse things than this." He threw it across to Eystein, who glanced at it, then flung it down the line of Varangers so that they should see it too.

The Protostrator watched this in horror. He said, "Ten goldsmiths worked all night to make this for you, captain. It is the new Order of Catalactus, created in your honour, and you are the first to wear it."

Harald went back to his lacing. He said, "I shall not wear it, my friend, make no mistake. It will go into my coffer with the other pretty things and one day will buy me a few longships when I go back to Norway. Tell your master that before we sail Georgios Maniakes should be given one of these things too. Otherwise he may think that I am being set above him and that would not do. Captains must be treated equally. That is my rule."

The High Chamberlain bit his lips but said, "We shall convey your thanks and your wise advice to the Most Serene Majesty."

Harald shrugged his shoulders. "The thanks do not matter," he said, "but the advice is of importance. Do not forget it."

And when they had gone away, frowning at the Norseman's ill manners, Harald turned to Wulf and said, "Well, brother, did I not tell you to be more charitable in your judgements? As you see now, this emperor is a pleasant little fellow who only wishes to make friends with us."

10 · The Sailing

Later that day the emperor's galleys set sail westward through the Sea of Marmora towards the Hellespont. By special imperial dispensation Harald was allowed to sail in *Stallion* and Eystein Baardson in *War Hawk*, though they had had to be repainted in the Byzantine purple for this occasion. This disgusted the Northmen, who believed that the proper colour for a longship was black and no other.

The high-pooped and gilded galley of Maniakes went first with Hardrada's longship three cable-lengths after it. Then followed the Greeks and the Varangers sailing in line astern, parallel to each other so that neither should feel insulted.

The sunlit air was full of the high screaming of silver trumpets. The people of Byzantium, in great crowds on the walls, thought they had never seen so many flags and banners and pennants before. It was as though the whole blue sea was aflame with jewels. They felt proud to be Greeks once more.

And when the fleet had come out into more open water the trumpets howled again and steersmen pulled hard upon their helms so that the two lines arranged themselves abreast behind their leaders. An old man on the Marble Tower by the inner wall saw this and cried out, "Look, look! They are going to sweep all the seas of the world clear for us. Now the barbarians shall learn what it is to be a Greek!"

One of the Bulgars who were now left in charge of the city snarled at this and pushed the old man away from the parapet with the butt-end of his lance. He said, "Why, you old sheep, can you not see that Catalactus is just getting rid of a few hundred battle-crazy fools so that he can let some air into this fusty city, so that he can make some changes that have needed making for a thousand years?"

The old man muttered, "If he makes too many changes in the Holy City he will not last long on this earth."

He did not speak his thoughts aloud because he did not know whose side this fiercely bearded Bulgar was on.

But there was one watcher of this sailing who did not think that the Varangers were fools. She had been up since dawn at her high balcony praying for a glimpse of Hardrada—only a glimpse of one instant, no more. And she had seen him stride down to the wharfside with Haldor and Wulf on either side of him, and Eystein and Gyric behind him, all bearing their great axes over their shoulders, their golden hair floating behind them in the breeze that swept up from the sea.

When she had been granted such a sight she fell to her knees and prayed for them to come back safely. She promised to go without food or water for three days if God would let them come back unharmed. If she had known, she was to go without food and water for three days anyway since this was the lady Theodora's decree.

Of course Harald did not know this. Indeed his travel-hungry mind was filled with nothing but the journey in hand. He saw the great crowds of folk upon the walls, cheering and shouting, but such things meant little to him for he knew well enough that if ever he fell from favour those same crowds would jeer and snarl down at him from the high-tiered seats of the Hippodrome as the torturers went to work on him.

Once as his eagle eyes swept over the city he was about to leave, he did notice for an instant a small black-robed girl with a white face, on her knees and seeming to pray from a balcony. But Byzantium was full of black-robed people praying at all times of the day and night, so this sight caused him no concern.

He went down to the ships as gay as a spring lark.

11 · The Corsairs

After the first week time hung heavy over the Northmen and they wished that there was more to do than row and haul sails and gaze across the dazzling water at the dusty land on either side of them. Sometimes to amuse themselves they shouted insults at the Greek galleys nearest them, hoping that their allies would pull alongside and challenge them to fight. But when Harald got to hear of this he called to all the Varangers down a speaking-horn of leather, warning them to save their energies for fighting their enemies and not their friends.

From time to time he would go aboard the galley of

Georgios Maniakes and noticed that the Greek general always wore his new Order of Catalactus over his gilded breastplate. When the general once asked Harald where his chain was the Norseman answered, "In safe enough keeping. It is not our custom to wear jewellery into battle." He said no more and after that Maniakes ceased to wear his gold chain.

Once they had passed through the Hellespont and out into the broad Aegean they came up with a small fishing smack early one morning and hemmed it in before it could make off. They dragged the dark-faced fisherman aboard a galley and asked him the news of those parts. But the man was so terrified that he was struck dumb at first. So Haldor offered him a cup of wine and a piece broken from a barley loaf; and then the man began to talk very fast in a language that the Varangers could not understand. Maniakes sent one of his Greek lieutenants aboard *Stallion* to find out what was happening. This soldier listened to the fisherman for a while, then said, "He is deceiving us by speaking in the ancient dialect of Lemnos, using words that old Jason himself would have spoken in our forefathers' time. But he is as Greek as I am, gentlemen. You will see, when I have slit his tongue with my sharp dagger, he will talk as well as Michael Catalactus himself."

The man watched wide-eyed while the soldier drew out his dagger, and as soon as it came near to his mouth he began to talk like a true Byzantine. The Northmen heard this and thought it a great jest.

The fisherman said, "Mercy, lord, mercy. I did not dare to speak, not because I am your enemy, but because the pirates who infest our island would murder me if they thought I had told you where they have their lair."

The lieutenant then said, "You have told us what we wanted to know, you miserable coward. And now because you have insulted the General Maniakes himself by your gibbering, I shall do as I said earlier and shall slit your tongue."

The man fell to his knees and began to cry out to the Virgin for help. But Harald came forward and said to him, "There is no need to go as high as that, man, when your plea could be answered at a lower level. Now be quiet and behave yourself. Less of this bawling."

Then he turned to the lieutenant and said, "Put up your dagger, soldier. We know what we need to know."

The officer did so with a bad grace and went back to his general to report what Hardrada had said. Maniakes stormed about his deck in fury for a while, then sent a sailor to the side to call out that the fisherman's smack should be sunk. But once more Harald answered and called back, "If that little boat is sunk I shall see to it that three galleys go down beside it to keep it company."

Then the general's galley drew away as fast as the oars could beat; and the Northmen gave the fisherman a gold coin or two and another cup of wine, then dropped him into his smack and told him to be off while he was still whole. He thanked them until he was out of range of their arrows, then stood up in his boat and began to call them swine, dogs, hairy apes and white-eyed wolves.

Harald smiled and said, "Let him go. At least he has told us what we are. I was coming to the conclusion after all our time in the city that we were only wooden dolls."

Later that day they drew a cordon round the southern shore of Lemnos and found five low-lying galleys that belonged to pirates. They stove them all in with iron hooks, then went ashore in several waves and fetched out a score of rough-looking men who carried weapons. In the fighting two Greeks and one Norman were killed. Maniakes sat in judgement on the corsairs and gave a stern punishment. From pine trees he hanged four pirates for each Greek killed and two for the Norman. Harald did not like this judgement but he knew that the general had the Law of Byzantium on his side and that to contest this sentence would be an act of mutiny. Since this would bring death on all the Varangers when they got back to port, he turned away and let the punishment take place. But he saw to it that none of his own men hauled on the ropes. He also saw to it that the remaining pirates were turned loose that night, to make what escape they could.

For, as he said to Eystein Baardson, "I have a certain friendly feeling towards these rough fellows. I think I can understand how their minds work. I have been a sort of pirate myself in my time."

Eystein nodded and said, "I was once on the end of a rope in Clontarf for a similar thing, and I should have been eagle's meat by now but for another Orkneyman who sailed into harbour just as they were about to hoist me."

Wulf smiled and said, "See what a good man the world would have lost then!"

12 · Wulf's Kinsman

Months passed and the Byzantine fleet swept down the Aegean like a great coloured broom. It was more a fishing fleet than a sea-army, for its wide-spread net caught all but the smallest craft that could slip through the mesh. Often towards sunset the Varangers saw the larger black Corsairs driving on southwards towards Crete or Rhodes, rather than stay and be dragged in.

By the late summer the Greek galleys were low on the water-line with taxes and pirate-plunder, since it was the rule that Varangers might not take such official loot on board—in case they changed their allegiance at the last moment and took the lot home to the north.

In general the Northmen were there to fight and not to gather gold and since there was little fighting done they had much time to waste. Indeed, it became the rule for the Greek vessels to swing away from them at dawn on their own affairs and only to fetch them in to form a unified fleet if there was trouble. This they did by the use of flares sent up on the points of arrows, composed of nitre and saltpetre and other chemicals which the Byzantines had learned from the Arabs to use to form their own peculiar "Greek Fire".

So, unless there was such an alarm, the Varangers drew their ships alongside in batches by sundown and gathered together to talk about this and that. On Harald's ship only the most experienced warmen gathered and so they often talked of fighting and of death.

One evening when the stars shone through the dark indigo sky like pin-pricks in a lantern shield, a group of Norsemen sat round the log fire that Harald always had built in an iron grid on his deck. And Eystein said, "Men grow big by suffering."

This was the sort of thing that always started an argument among the Norwegians and Icelanders. The Danes and Swedes often snorted and frowned and spoke of something else, such as pig-breeding or market-prices in Gotland. But on this evening a big Swede said, "You dare to say that! You from the islands of sheep-manure and gulls' droppings?"

Haldor stepped in calmly and said, "He has the right to say anything that the Hardrada lets him, Swede. I come from Iceland—which even you may have heard of—and up there we have as many sheep and gulls as Orkney ever had or will have. I can see that your hand is creeping towards your axe but that does not trouble me. Two of my friends stand directly behind you, waiting for you to lift it—then you will know no more."

The big Swede looked round quite pleasantly and saw Wulf and Gyric with their hands on their weapons. So he said, "I am by nature an enquiring man, Haldor Snorreson, and the motion of my hand towards my axe only showed my great interest in the conversation. But I think you are a liar and a fool and will be prepared to demonstrate both to you if I may, and without the persuasion of your friends who stand directly behind me."

Haldor said, "By all means. When and where you like, Swede."

So the Swede said, "How can men grow big by suffering, when wounds, which you cannot call anything else but suffering, often chop them to a shorter length? For example, there was an uncle of mine called Glam, who stood as tall as or taller than your captain Harald. Now, he sailed up to Iceland when he was a brisk voyager looking for free forage, and got to be the bailiff of a farm . . . I forget where it was."

Wulf said from behind him with grim jaws, "It was in Shadyvale and the farmer's name was Thorhall."

The Swede turning, smiled at him and nodded. "You are right, Icelander," he said, "but so you should be, it was your country and it only happened fifteen years ago."

Haldor smiled back as starkly and said, "I too am from Iceland. I have heard the tale as often as Wulf has. Speak on."

Then the Swede, who had been drinking too much of the voyage ale, rubbed his long red nose and said, "This kinsman of mine called Glam was a pretty enough man in his day. Though he could make no living in our own land he did well enough in Iceland among the fools there, jumping out from behind barns by night and scaring rich farmer-chiefs; or trampling on the roof-thatch in the small hours and driving away the peasants. So in a few months he had more gold in his coffer than most of the Icelanders had. And all because of his great Swedish wit, you see."

Eystein suddenly said, "I can see the end of this story and

when it is told I hope that all men whose kinsmen are not involved should stand well away from this fire."

Most of the Varangers moved at these words. The Swede watched them go and then he said gently, "And when my uncle was well set towards becoming a rich man in his own right and was thinking of journeying back to Sweden to start his own farm and to raise his own family, along comes a brisk and blunt youth with a short sword in his hand to rid the land of its monster."

Wulf said, "Where did this youth come from, Swede?"

With unblinking lashless eyes the Swede said calmly, "He came from Biarg. Is there anything else you would like to know?"

Wulf shook his head, then jumped into the fire-glow swiftly with his sword in his right hand and his cloak wrapped round his left. He said, "No, thank you, Swede. His name was Grettir, he was my mother's brother and he shortened your troll of a kinsman by a head's length."

The Swede rose too, grinning whitely, his axe up over his shoulder. "Aye, that is what I am driving at, Icelander," he said.

The men scattered. But just then Hardrada came from his after-cabin and kicked the hearth-fire into the sea and the deck was in darkness.

No man saw exactly what happened; but later when Gyric lit the lamps both Wulf and the Swede were lying side by side with puffed eyes and swelled noses, their sword and axe well away from them, not boasting about anything but only snoring.

And in the morning Harald got the Varanger ships hooked together and held a great Council on the sea, just off Naxos, in which he said: "Whether we are Norwegians, Swedes, Icelanders, Danes, Normans, or even English—we are of the one blood. And I will not see that good blood spilled on foreign waters unless there is a bargain to be gained by it from these dark-eyed Greeks. So understand from this time, if I see any one of you—even my dearest friend—as much as raise a clenched fist to strike another of the northern brothers, then his head upon a wooden platter will be the cheapest way he can avoid my wrath."

And when he had finished shouting all this down the leather horn he ordered the ships to be cast away. Then he went down to where Wulf lay groaning and, feeling his jaw to find how many teeth he had lost, he said starkly but gently, "Wulf Ospakson, do I, or do I not, love my right hand?"

Wulf mumbled that Harald loved his right hand.

Then Harald said, "But if that hand was full of venom from a viper's bite what would I do?"

Wulf waited long before answering; but in the end, with Hardrada staring at him, he had to answer and he said, "You would cut it off, brother."

Harald nodded like a hairy dragon and said, "And why would I cut it off, brother?"

Wulf gulped and said, "So that the poison did not rot all your body, captain."

Then Harald said, "So, dear Wulf, when I have a body like this fleet about me, do you wonder that I wish to cut off any part which might poison it?"

Wulf even expected death then, so he gave up trying to excuse himself and lay back with his arms wide and the neck of his shirt open to make it easier for his leader.

He said with his eyes closed, "I have often wondered what it was like to be dead, Harald. Men say so many different things, you can't tell what is true or what is false. So in a way I am not sorry. I shall know before quite a number of men about me know."

There was a heavy silence hanging over his eyelids that lasted for a long while. In fact Wulf went to sleep during that silence. And when he opened his eyes again Harald had gone.

So Wulf did not get to know what death was like at that time. Although he tried hard enough to find out, one way and another, as the voyage went on.

13 · Goose-woman and Quarrel

Now when they got down to the shore at Naxos and found that here they had space for all to drive their galleys on to the sand and clear their undersides of weed and barnacles, Maniakes decided that the fleet should stay for a while.

The northern sea-folk were quicker than the Greeks at carrying out their work and then looked round for something else to do. A Greek lieutenant who had been a scholar before he took to carrying arms said, "Go up above the snow-line among the pines and from there you will get a fine view across the sea. As you look northwards tell yourselves that this is the sea-route old Theseus took on his way back from Crete."

Harald said, "This Theseus killed the bull, as well as being a good seaman. I am always ready to stand where old heroes have stood."

So he took his three friends and they went up in the evening sun. And when they got among the trees they saw a tumble-down cabin roofed with pine-boughs, and a very old woman dressed in black sitting before the hanging door, watching four geese cropping the grass.

When she caught sight of the Northmen, bare-headed, bare-legged, in their tunics of white linen because of the heat, she cried out to Harald, "So at last you have come back to fetch me after all those years. The folk down below told me you would never come, but I prayed to Mother Dia and even to Pallas Athene since she looks over your city; and here you are."

Harald bowed before her with courtesy and said, "I admire the pretty coronet of ivy about your head, lady."

She began to laugh and answered, "I still have a flask of the purple wine we drank that day, we Maenads, when you sailed away and left me among the raving women. Would you care to taste it, bull-leaper?"

Harald saw inside that dirty cottage and saw too that her clothes and hands and face were not of the cleanest. So he bowed again and said, "I did not drink it then and I shall not drink it now. But, all with respect, my lady."

She laughed and said, "Why do you call me 'lady'? It sounds so formal. Once you called me Ariadne."

This meant nothing to Harald, whose mind was taken up with the business of escaping from this sad old woman who lived alone in the wood. So he said, to pass the time, "And how are your family, Ariadne?"

Among Northmen this was a question that one would ask the merest stranger; but the old woman began to tear at her black dress in anger then and shouted out, "You know well enough how they are. My father died of grief when your ruffians sacked his city; and my sister hanged herself when her love for you turned her mind. Do not ask me how my family is; there are none of them left, you sly Athenian."

Wulf put a little bag of coin beside her and they almost ran back down through the pine-wood. They knew that she threw the coins after them for they heard them clinking against the tree-trunks as they went.

Haldor was for stopping to pick them up but Harald told him: "Leave them be, you fool. If we stay we shall have a mad woman on our hands."

Down at the shore again they told the young Greek lieutenant what they thought of him for sending them up there.

He only laughed in a sort of mockery and then passed the story round. Soon General Maniakes came to Harald and said, "Lead me to this old woman. She needs care so I will have her put into the gaol-house down here in the village where the folk can keep an eye on her."

But Harald shook his head and said, "She is well enough where she lives, Maniakes. Do not meddle."

The general tugged at his beard, for this was said before the men; and from this small happening a greater quarrel came before dark.

It was like this: the whole army of men saw that night was coming on and so decided to pitch tents on Naxos before sailing the next day. Now the site chosen by the captains lay near the pine-wood, which would give shelter from the blustery winds of that season and so the men set off up the hill. The Northmen, being more active than the Greeks, reached this spot first and began to pitch their tents on the highest ground. They had hardly driven in their main poles when Georgios Maniakes stumped up and said, "So, you Northmen insist on defying me at every turn. You insist on picking the hard high ground for yourselves, leaving my countrymen to lie in the damp grass lower down the hill. I command you to move straightway. We, the Greeks of Byzantium, will have this site."

Now Harald came forward, his red face set, and he said, "I think that there is some mistake in your argument, Maniakes. First, we Varangers serve the emperor and the empress as well as you do and so are equally privileged. Second, my men will take orders from none but me, as is our arrangement. Third, throughout this voyage it has been our custom for whoever gets there first to choose his place for sleeping. All armies do this; I am asking for nothing strange. Finally, we have never asked your Greeks to shift their tent-poles once they were up, whatever advantage they had found for themselves. You see,

Maniakes, all good soldiers must fend for themselves. That is the nature of their trade. So if your Greeks are slow off the mark that is their misfortune. My men will not shift their tents any more than they would expect you to shift yours, once set on the ground."

He began to turn away but Maniakes went white with fury and laid his hands on Harald and swung him round before all the men. He shouted out, "You, why you Norse swineherd, you do not deserve to live."

He was a brave man, though a stupid one, and even began to wrench at his sword. Harald shrugged his shoulders and laid his own right hand on that of Maniakes, making it impossible for the general to draw his weapon.

When the Varangers saw this, they gritted their teeth and got out their own swords, in case their captain needed help—though they hardly thought this likely. Then the hot-tempered Greeks began to shout out that this was their land and that they would die rather than let rough Outlanders have the better of them. So they got out their swords and came up the hill in anger.

Harald was the first to see that this affair could only end in the loss of many good men. So he swallowed his pride and his sense of justice and said to Maniakes, "So be it. We will make a new rule to fit the occasion since you will not stick to the ancient one. We will each put our mark on a piece of tree-bark and throw them into a helmet. Then we will get one of your Greeks to draw a piece out; if he draws yours, then your army shall have the upper ground, and gladly. If he draws mine, then my Varangers shall stay where they are. Does that content you?"

By then the general's fury had abated a little and not to seem childish he had to nod his head and to agree.

So Harald marked his piece of bark with a raven, wings outspread, which was his banner-sign; and Maniakes marked his with a Christian cross, and they threw the two lots into a helmet.

Then they blindfolded the Greek lieutenant and told him to put his hand into the helmet and to take one piece out. When this man held up the lot he had drawn, Harald laughed and striding to him snatched it from his hand and threw it into the air. The night wind took it and swept it out over the cliff and down into the sea.

Maniakes stamped with rage at this but Harald said calmly, "Why will you always show the men your worst side, general? There still remains one piece of bark in the helmet. Take it, look at it, and announce to us all whose it is—for that piece will decide who is to camp lower down the hill. That is as fair and just as the other way, is it not?"

So Georgios Maniakes plunged in his hand and savagely drew out the piece of bark. Then he looked at it but did not speak. "Go on, general," said Harald slyly. "The men are waiting for your golden words."

Then Maniakes was forced to call out so that all could hear, "The piece that remains is marked with a cross."

And Harald asked smoothly, "And what does that mean, general?"

Then grim-faced Maniakes said, "You all know well enough. It means that the Greeks camp lower down the hill."

So Harald said sweetly, "Then there is no problem, general." And turning to the Varangers he shouted, "Carry on, men. Leave the poles where they are. The general agrees to our position on the hill."

But the face of Maniakes became as furious as before. Under his breath he said to Harald, "You may think that you have bested me this time, Norseman, but watch out with both your eyes in the future for I do not take any insult lightly. Before long I shall find a way to make you eat humble pie—and to pretend that you enjoy the meal."

Then he stumped off down the hill to his men. Harald held up his hand to his men to stop them from laughing. It was never his custom to belittle any man more than was strictly necessary.

14 · Battle Plans

The Byzantine army wintered on Cyprus where the climate was good. There the two leaders had many quarrels over one thing and another but they did not come to blows; and always Harald seemed to come out on top, though he made nothing of it.

And when the spring came, after they had tarred their boats, Maniakes said to Harald, "It was an easy game, clearing the Greek Sea of a few miserable pirates. Now it is my wish that we take our men to a place where we shall find real work to test them."

Harald nodded. "The Varangers have never been known to turn back from anything they have set their hands to, Maniakes," he answered. "Where a Greek can go, there you will find a Northman. Where shall we try our luck next then?"

Maniakes ground his teeth and said, "Into the lands stolen by the Turks, Varanger. We will land at Antioch and then make our way to Aleppo and afterwards along the Euphrates valley. So there will always be water for the men. A good captain always thinks first of his men."

Harald smiled, "I have led men long enough to have learned that lesson, Maniakes," he said. "But tell me more, shall we sack Bagdad while we are about it?"

The general stamped about his tent and then said, "Are you

a madman? Our emperor has a pact with the caliph. We must not touch Bagdad."

Harald said, "My question was an innocent one. I am a soldier, not a pact-maker. I am not to know whether the emperor has made pacts or has broken them."

The general swung on him in fury and said, "His Most Serene Majesty never breaks a pact. Are you a traitor to suggest such a thing? If you had said that to me in Byzantium, before witnesses, I would have had you punished."

Harald nodded and answered, "Aye, little one, you would have had your Bulgars throw me into a cow-pen—and would then have regretted it later."

From this meeting they did not part the best of friends.

At sundown Georgios Maniakes called all his lieutenants to him in private and told them: "These Varangers are getting to be a thorn in my flesh. I cannot stand their insolence much longer. Now look, we are about to embark on a most dangerous enterprise and many who are alive and laughing today will lie stark in the deserts with carrion-birds about them before we turn our faces back towards the Holy City. For my own part I would rather the vultures picked at Northmen than at Greeks. So in all our battle plans from now on I shall regard it as my duty to the emperor to place these Varangers where they stand the best chance of feeding the birds. Is that understood?"

The lieutenants nodded solemnly. All of them wanted promotion so there was nothing else they could do but agree with their general.

Gyric of Lichfield was passing the back of Maniakes' tent when this was arranged and though he lacked an eye there was nothing wrong with his ears. He went to Harald and told what he had heard. The Varanger smiled and clapped him on the back. "Forewarned is forearmed, friend," he said. "So we must see to it that these crafty Greeks do not make eagle-fodder out of us. I for one would like to see Trondheim again. I have recently had the desire to build a church there; the one they have is a tumbledown old wooden thing and now that I have seen a few churches in Byzantium I have a good idea how we could improve on ours up north."

Gyric said, "I am not one for churches. That is your affair, Harald. I am concerned about battles."

Harald laughed and said, "Aye, Mercian, and so am I. Leave this to me and I will see that these Greeks do not feed us to the Turks. This general must be taught that Northmen fight their own sort of battle and not one that is thrust upon them. From this time, thanks to your timely warning, our plan will be to give value to the emperor in Byzantium—whatever we think of him—but to come scot-free from all battles. And if we have to leave a few Greeks behind, well, that is their bad luck."

Gyric smiled and said, "I could not have put it better my-self, Harald."

And Harald said, "You deceive yourself, Englishman—you could not have put it half so well!"

Then they both laughed and put their great arms round one another in a warrior's grip—which resembled the hugging of bears more than anything else.

15 · The Turcopoles

On the third day out from Aleppo, the army with its requisitioned horses and baggage-wagons, got in lease with the ships in security, came to a small green valley that led down to the Euphrates. And here they stayed to eat and drink. Camp kitchens were set up and horse-lines laid out. The two regiments positioned themselves separately.

And when they were in the middle of their feeding, a cloud of dust suddenly rose on the hill above them and a hundred lancemen in white robes and turbans came bearing down towards them. Most of the Varangers and all of the Greeks had their body-armour off, since the weather had turned warm and sultry. Harald shouted to his folk, "Only the helmet! Only the helmet! There is no time for anything else. Form what sort of hedge you can, in three ranks. All the best axe-men in the first rank. And you others, watch where you strike with your longswords; there might be a comrade under it. Only hit the dark-faced ones."

Then he looked round and smiled broadly. "Have we any Arabs among us?" he said. The flax-haired Varangers laughed back at this and ran to get into triple rank. One of them, a tall thin beanpole of a man from Shetland, whose hair was as white as snow although he was only nineteen, yelled back, "Aye, Hardrada, I am an Arab. Didn't you know?"

Harald heard this and shouted, "Right, Muslim. Come to my tent later and I will pay you double-fee for marching with these Norse rogues."

Then the horsemen slithered to a halt, spurting up so much dust that they could hardly be seen; and their emir got off his mount and came striding down in his great flapping cloak, laughing. "By the Virgin," he said, "but we thought you were Egyptians, the way you sit down with never a care, to eat and drink in the bad lands."

Harald was first to him, leaving Maniakes far behind, and said to the leader, "Then who, by the White Christ, are you?"

The Arab said smiling, "We are the emperor's Turcopoles, Englishman. We are foraging for what we can find out here, although we are supposed to stay round the port to keep it clear. But who can blame a soldier for looking beside the way for a little profit?"

Harald answered, "Not I, for one, but I must blame you for

calling me an Englishman. I have nothing against that folk, but let it be known I am a Norwegian."

The Arab smiled with white teeth and said, "To us, you all look the same. Moreover you sound the same. But if you choose to call yourself by another name, that is your right."

Harald agreed that it was, and then asked the man if his pay was coming through well from Byzantium.

The Arab shook his head. "My cavalry have not seen a Byzant for over three months," he said. "If old Zoë knows her business she will get something out to us before long, or the young ones in the squadrons will start to remember Mahomet again and will go north to join the Turks."

Harald said, "I will send such a message back to the Holy City when I have the chance. In the meanwhile will you come to my pavilion and drink a cup of ale with me since you are a Christian?"

But at that moment Maniakes caught up with them and said in fury, "This man is not a Greek to be offered hospitality, Varanger. He is a paid servant of the Most Serene Majesty, no more. Tell him to take his flea-bitten horsemen back to Aleppo where he should be, and to earn his pay as a soldier should."

The emir stood away and drew in his lips. He looked from one captain to another. Then he bowed rather too elaborately and said, "As you will, Greek. But let it be known that we are no servants, we Turcopoles. We are the equal of any Greek. And our Christianity is as sound, if not sounder. Let it also be known that we have paraded out here in the desert for over three months, living on what we could find, like jackals, and with never a single coin from the Holy City to put food into our mouths."

Maniakes cried out, "Complain in the proper quarters, Turcopole. It is no business of mine. Now get back to your patrol."

The emir saluted in a casual way, almost insolently. Then he turned and went back to his waiting horsemen and mounted. Soon he called down into the valley, "I will take your advice, Greek. I will complain in the proper quarters since you Byzantines are so set on your own destruction. But if those quarters happen to look towards Mecca and not Constantine's old village, don't blame me, you whey-faced donkey."

The Varangers thought this a good description and lost no time in laughing at it and in cheering the brave emir. For his part, he bowed from the high saddle with a grave face towards them, then slowly turned and cantered back to his glowering men.

Harald said, "You have made a needless enemy there, Maniakes."

The general flared out at him: "Who asked you? Get back to your own folk, too. You are no better."

Harald stood a while, wondering whether to strike the man between the two hosts. Then he shrugged his shoulders. "Little Georgios," he said, "whoever sent you out with all these men under your command did ill. They should have kept you back in the imperial palace there, with a black wand in your hand, guiding visitors in to see old Theodora. At least you know the way to that black crow's cell."

Then he turned his back on the general and walked steadily towards his people. Maniakes started to tug at his swords, then stopped, wiped his streaming face, and swung away to his Greeks, cursing the day he had ever agreed to come out on an expedition with Norsemen.

16 · Harald's Pact

That night almost as soon as the moon went down there was a great thrumming of hooves, a terrible thundering of kettle-drums, a deep hollow whirring of hornbow strings; and the camp in the green valley was in a desperate condition.

Wulf ran outside his tent and straightway found himself floundering among the wild lavender with a short bolt through his thigh. When he tried to get it out the pain from the blunt pile nearly sent him into a faint, so he called softly to Haldor to come out, on hands and knees, and to give him a hand.

Haldor came and got his bolt in the left shoulder. He lowered himself to that hard ground and said between tight teeth, "Only an Icelander-idiot would call his friend out just now."

But Wulf was beyond answering and only groaned in the purple dusk.

Harald heard all this, coming out of his deep sleep. So taking up his shield like a cautious warman, he held it over his head as he bent under the tent-flap. Three bolts clanged over it before he reached his mates. He looked down at them and said, "If God had meant men to crawl on the earth like slugs He would not have given them legs. Come on, up with you Icelanders."

Then he bore them, groaning, back into the tent.

There he laid them on the beds and said, "This is a bad business, and that whey-faced donkey Maniakes is to blame for it."

He fetched in the Byzantine surgeon to attend to his friends, then slid low like an adder to the tent of Georgios

Maniakes. The General was fast asleep, so Harald hit him hard over the right ear, then put his hand tight over the Greek's mouth. Maniakes woke with the thud, sat up, tried to yell, found that the breath would not leave his mouth, and began to flail his limbs.

Harald said, "Do not take on so, general. It is only the Seljuks who are attacking us. A small thing to those who have been stung by Byzantine wasps!"

When he felt sure that the general had calmed down, he took his hand away and said, "Two of my best men are wounded. We are in a bad position, most of us being half-asleep and all of us being completely surrounded. In future I mean to choose our camping-places, for it is no sort of sense to lie in a valley where the enemy can shoot down on to us like this."

Georgios Maniakes sat up in his pallet-bed and said, "A mistake can be made by anyone. My scouts told me that the nearest Seljuks were fifty miles away."

"Then we must thrash the scouts," said Harald, "for they should also have told you that Seljuks will ride all night to catch their prey."

"Let us have done with this talk," answered the general, reaching for his helmet and swords, "and form into some sort of battle order to meet them."

Harald reached over and took the two swords tightly in his grasp. "You will not be using these tonight, Maniakes," he said. "If we try to meet them, in whatever order, they will send up flares and then pick us off as we scramble up the slopes."

Maniakes loathed to see his swords in another man's hand, especially this man's, and he shivered with fury. At last he said, "So you fly your true colours now, Norseman, and declare yourself to be a coward who will not fight for the pay his master gives him."

Harald threw the swords to the far side of the tent and said, "I declare myself to be a man of craft, not stupidity, Greek. Your emperor would need to pay me as much as he has in his imperial treasury before I would go charging at Seljuks by night. I have a strong wish to reach the old age of forty, and that I should never do if I went out as a warman now."

Georgios Maniakes glared at him. "What then are we to do, O wise Norwegian?" he asked in mockery.

Harald said, "You are to lie down again like a quiet peaceful man, and I will go up the hill in my shirt, with no war gear, to talk to these Turks. But one thing is sure, I will not have another single man of mine stuck with arrows because of your foolish pride."

Then he went outside, running under cover of the many tents and hearing the short arrows smack into them as he went. In his own pavilion he tied a length of white cloth on to a staff and took a horn in his other hand.

Like this he went outside, blowing the horn so that the Turks should see that he wished them to notice him, and waving the white flag like a pedlar calling the folk to his market-stall. Three arrows narrowly missed him and then he heard a stern order from the hilltop. After this all arrows ceased to whirr in the darkness. A great red and yellow flare was lit to show him where to go, so Harald went in that direction.

And when he was at the top of the slope, he saw a band of white-clad horsemen, with stout mail under their cloaks and swords every bit as good as anything he had seen in the north. They seemed to cluster round a tall man who wore both black and white, and sat on a lithe pony with silver trappings. Harald went towards this man and said, "I am Harald Sigurdson, whom men call Hardrada."

The leader on the horse bowed his head and smiled. "We are aware of that," he said in very good camp Greek, "otherwise we should not have allowed you to come up here to us. I am

Abu Firuz, Scourge of Aleppo as simple men call me, and I have three hundred horsemen about this valley."

Harald said, "From the noise they have been making, I thought there must be more. But we will not discuss that since it is in my mind that you would be wasting quite a number of them if you came down into the valley at close quarters and met my Varangers. And I, for my part, would be a stupid fellow if I let my brave comrades try to sink their northern fangs into your host. I will not say that the score is even for we can both see that an army caught in a valley is at a disadvantage."

Abu Firuz listened to him courteously, nodding, then said, "What are we to do then, Harald Sigurdson?"

Harald leaned on his staff and smiled. "I have never been one to run away from a fight if I thought there was honour to be gained in staying; but if we fought tonight there would be no honour for either of us, Scourge of Aleppo. We must come to an arrangement, as sensible men always do when their anger has died down. Now, as you can see in the light of this flare, I am not angry; and, from your own smiling, I observe that you are not, either."

Abu Firuz got down from his pony and stood by Harald. His head came up to the Northman's shoulder, but in all other ways he was a most proper man and a true, hawk-nosed warrior. He said, "Let us go to my tent and talk of this."

It was the richest tent Harald had seen, with its samite hangings and carpets and cushions set on the ground for them to sit on. And there Harald and Abu Firuz drank a cup of sherbet in which floated pieces of ice. Harald said laughing, "This is not the sort of drink that would turn a man's head, but at this time of such a warm night I can think of no pleasanter wine."

The Seljuk shook his head. "It is not wine, Sigurdson," he said. "We do not drink wine. Now, what arrangement are we to make, we two?"

Harald scratched his shaggy head and said, "I cannot offer you any sort of ransom since I have no coin or loot with me. Maniakes, my fellow captain, has sent all that back to the emperor. We Varangers carry only what we need for making war."

The Seljuk Turk rubbed his chin and then said thoughtfully, "Are you offering, then, to bring your Northmen over to our side? Is that the arrangement you were thinking of?"

Harald said, "I have no doubt that we should enjoy that much more than fighting alongside these Greeks; but unfortunately I have sworn an oath to serve the emperor in Greekland, and an oath is an oath, as you know."

Abu Firuz nodded then and answered, "I am glad that you think so. If you had offered to betray your master by riding with us, I should have had no alternative but to kill you now for, of all the sins, disloyalty in a soldier is the worst. Very well, what are we to do?"

Harald said, "This has come to my mind. From now on until we are well outside your territory, I swear to you that we Varangers will molest no one, will sack no city and will shed no blood."

Abu considered this, then asked, "But what of your Greek companions? What of your general? Will he agree to this?"

Harald smiled ruefully and said, "You know as well as I do, Abu Firuz, that this Maniakes is a famous soldier who is unlikely to follow the advice of a Varanger captain. I have no doubt that he will storm and fret and stamp about the place; but if we from the north do not join him in battle there is little he can do, save tear out his hair and beard in rage. He has not enough men under him to cause your people any great discomfort. Is this a bargain?"

Abu Firuz looked at him narrowly and said, "And you do not consider this to be disloyalty?"

Harald laughed aloud. "Why no, "he said, "because as soon as we have passed through your own land towards Mosul, say, my men will fight as fiercely as ever alongside their Greek fellows."

Abu Firuz nodded and said, "I am not sure that I understand your northern reasoning completely, Harald, but I will draw off my army provided that you agree to two points which I shall make. First, that you shall explain in detail to the general Maniakes what we have said together; and secondly that you leave behind in the valley one wagon-load of provisions. My riders travel lightly and at present are lacking in food. So you would be doing me a favour by agreeing."

Harald stood up and held out his right hand for the Turk to grasp. But Abu Firuz said, "We do not seal our bargains in your manner, Harald. Think it no disgrace that I do not take your hand. What we will do is to have a scribe come in and make two copies of the words we have spoken. You shall have one and I the other. Can you write your name?"

Harald shrugged his shoulders and answered, "Usually someone does that for me and I make a raven beside the name, for that is my sign."

"Then," said Abu Firuz, "that is what we will do now. There is a Frankish scribe among us and he will see that all is done correctly."

And that is how the Byzantine army came out of the green valley alive. Though Georgios Maniakes went into such a fury that he lay ill in a litter for three days afterwards as they passed on towards Mosul.

The wounds of Wulf and Haldor healed quickly, for they were hardy men; besides, Abu Firuz sent his own physician down to them with medicines and salves before the Christian armies went away.

But Maniakes did not hide his annoyance at Harald's pact with the Saracens. As soon as he could, he sent a messenger northwards towards Sinope, to give the emperor Michael Catalactus a complete account of Harald's treachery.

17 · The Wall of Mosul

Things did not go too well along the desert route towards Mosul. The old man who styled himself emir there lay on a sick-bed, weakened by malaria and dysentery, and so the city was in the hands of his eldest son, a fierce young man named Kamil who hated all Christians and especially Greeks. To him came the insulted Turcopoles with their grievance, and he promised to give them all their outstanding pay if they saw to it that the Byzantines were weakened before they reached the city.

So day by day the army of Maniakes had to put up with the harrying of the horsemen, who swept out of the blinding dust without warning and loosed off volleys of arrows at them before galloping away. Now the Byzantines were forced to wear their heavy hauberks, with the thick quilted coats beneath them, even on the hottest day. As food supplies ran out, some of them killed their horses and ate them. So they plodded along, heavily armed, on foot, often with so many short Turkish arrows sticking out of their padded coats that they looked more like hedgehogs than men.

To add to their discomfort Kamil ordered that all the wells along that route should be poisoned, stained with dyes, or defiled with the carcasses of dead sheep. And finally, to make all worse, half-way to Mosul the Byzantine host came across a swarming encampment of Bedouin who claimed to be converted Christians and so insisted on protection.

Maniakes tried to turn them away, but these folk, with their multitude of women, children and even dogs, goats and camels, insisted on following in the wake of the army and in sharing whatever food and drink there was.

Harald said to the general, "If I had my way I would threaten to fire their tents and eat their camels—little as I fancy that meat—unless they left us."

But the general said, "Our emperor would think ill of us for treating his Christian subjects in that way, Varanger. Nor will he think well of the man who suggested it."

So Harald gave up trying to make sense out of the situation; but privately he sent Eystein to the Bedouin headman with the stark message that if he was wise he would find some other way of putting food and drink into his people's mouths since the Northmen had now become weary of living on half-rations.

The Bedouin sent back the pleasant reply that when he and Harald met in Heaven he would put his complaints to God Himself.

When Harald heard this he flew into one of his strange furies and said, "When I find myself standing before the same God as that shrivelled thief, then I will swing myself into another tree. From now on if I hear of any Varanger sharing his food and drink with these unwashed scavengers, that man shall receive forty stripes with my sword-belt. That is my judgement."

From this, Wulf and Haldor saw that their brother was not himself, for his temper, though fiery when roused, was usually sailing on an even keel and not easily upset.

Then they came to Mosul. And when they saw its crumbling walls the Varangers began to wonder why they had come so far to sack this ruinous heap.

Yet as they walked towards the gate, shower after shower of arrows came over at them so quickly that they were forced back, leaving eight men down before the wall. Harald was so angry at this, he turned to where Maniakes stood with his lieutenants, well out of range on a little hilltop, and said, "I see that you are in no hurry to gain glory. Very well, with eight of my friends dead on the ground, I now regard this as a personal matter and shall be insulted if you send your Greeks in at this place. It shall be mine or no one's."

Maniakes answered with scorn, "There is a correct way of conducting a siege and you are not following it. However, if your mind is fixed on losing men, that is your affair. We shall withdraw half a mile and watch what you do. It is possible to learn something even from the most stupid of animals."

Now there was a man called Moriartak who claimed to be close kinsman to the King of Connaught. He was small and red-haired but among the Varangers there was no man more nimble. He had first gained fame up in Caithness on a foray, when he vaulted out of a burning barn in which he was trapped, on the end of a broomstick. Five other rovers, two heads taller than Moriartak but lacking his wit, stayed in that barn and were burned. Because of this he was called Moriartak Broomstick, and everyone in the north knew why. Any earl or chieftain from Iceland down to Galloway would have given him a place at the feast board just to hear his story of the barn-burning.

And this man came to Harald and said, "Captain, I have been looking at this wall. If I had a long stick, strong enough to bear my weight, I could run among the arrows, vault into Mosul, then open the gates and let you all into this city. It would make a great supper-story."

Harald said, "General Maniakes would grind his teeth if we carried out our siege in that farmyard manner."

Moriartak said, "General Maniakes can put his head in a bucket for all I care. Will you give me permission to go? You see, before I came southwards, I promised my mother and my sisters that I would bring great honour on our family by some other deed than merely jumping out of a northern cow-byre."

Harald said, "I have just lost eight men. I do not wish to lose a single one more. If we wait until dark we may all go against this place together and come off unscathed, because they cannot see to shoot arrows in the dark. No, I must refuse you, Moriartak. But thank you for offering."

Then the man stepped up close to Harald and said in a very strange voice, "I have a confession to make to you, captain. I hoped to keep this from you, but from the way my legs are now twitching I know that I must reveal my secret. Like my father and my three brothers who are all now under the ground, I am a baresark."

Harald drew him aside and said, "How long have you known this, little one?"

And Moriartak answered, "Since I was fifteen, when I went into the red dream and killed two tax-gatherers who were treating my mother badly while the grown men were away."

Harald said, "Well, a baresark is a baresark. Have you told the priest about this?"

Moriartak nodded and said, "In my youth my mother took me to ten priests, including a bishop, and though they sprinkled me with enough holy water to float a longship they all said that it was the will of God, and that there was no spell in the Book for the curing of my condition."

Then Harald patted the man on the back and said, "Well, what must be, must. Get yourself the best stick you can find, and then do what you mean to do. I will have two hundred Varangers just out of bowshot, waiting to run in the instant we see the gates moving. Good luck to you, baresark."

Later, all the Northmen watched the red-haired man go running towards the walls, zig-zagging so that the arrows all missed him, and shouting in the usual piercing high voice all the way to the walls. And when he reached them at their lowest point, they saw him give a great heave, then sail up into the air on his stick and over, out of sight.

Harald said, "Forward now, men, and keep your shields well up over your heads."

But though they waited an hour, the gates did not move, and so they drew back and sat outside the tents in a grim silence.

Towards dusk they saw a high siege catapult come slowly up on the other side of the wall, and shortly a heavy dark missile came whizzing over towards them. It fell into the largest of the camp fires and did no damage apart from scattering the embers.

Wulf said, "That was no stone."

Haldor said, "No, it is a hide bag. But there is nothing explosive in it. Get one of the men to drag it out of the fire with a grappling-hook and we will see what new ways of making war these Turks have nowadays."

And when they had opened the bag, they found in it the burned body of Moriartak, all in separate pieces. There was a strange smile on his face although his red hair was singed off.

Harald ground his teeth, then said, "So, he must come all that way from Caithness to die in the fire after all. The ways of God are hidden from us."

Eystein Baardson said, "Well, Moriartak never leaped so far before, and without the aid of a stick this time. Come on, Harald, let us take some vengeance for this."

Just then a messenger from General Maniakes came up and said, "Our master commands you to stay back, captain. He is now about to demonstrate the correct manner of taking a city."

Harald said to the man, "Go back and tell your master that we shall take this city in our own way without his aid. And tell him that if he moves as few as five men from your position on the hill, then the Varangers will come over and thrash you Greeks soundly in sight of the Turks."

The messenger stumped off haughtily and soon all the Greeks sat on the ground with their backs towards the Varangers and the city, as though disowning them.

Then Gyric of Lichfield came forward and said, "They are leaving it to us, Harald. We must see that we give them a good show, now that we have asked for it. What are we to do?"

Harald said, "We will choose the most crumbling piece of the wall and we will gather heaps of scrub wood from about us in the desert. When darkness comes at its thickest, ten of us will run forward with the brushwood and torches, and another ten will go beside them with hammers, chisels and axes. If there are any iron levers about, we will take them too. They could be very useful. And when we are under the wall, we will knock out as many stones as we can, near the ground, push in the brushwood and set light to it. Once the inner rubble and mortar have dried out, the wall will crack, and then sway,and then tumble. The rest of you must be ready to scramble over the stones and to fight your way to the emir's house. Do not waste your time and force by going anywhere else, and kill no more of the ordinary folk of this place than you have to. We shall need their good will when we are masters of Mosul."

This battle plan went without any hindrance. Ten yards of the wall came down before dawn, and when the first cocks crowed in the city, the Varangers were inside, with the loss of only two men dead and six wounded.

18 · The Greek Spy

After that it was harsh going up through the narrow alleys towards the inner citadel, but the Saracens were as hampered as the Varangers; and by a great stroke of good fortune a mule-drawn wagon got stuck in the citadel gates so that they could not close, and the Northmen were quickly inside.

They saw which was the emir's house by the great banner before it, marked with the crescent moon, and into this place they stormed shouting.

The courtyard was crowded with slaves, who fell to their knees and shrieked out for mercy. The Varangers passed by them and went into the rooms of the palace, looking for the emir. They found him in his bed reading the Koran and paying small attention to what was going on.

Harald said to him, "I beg pardon for interrupting your devotions, sir, but we are here on a matter of some urgency. Do you surrender this city to me?"

The emir said, "I am almost prepared to surrender everything, young man, for at my age the Will of Allah makes itself very apparent. If you will kneel before me and allow some of my captains into this chamber to bear witness, I will put the city in your hands for as long as Allah chooses to let you keep it. Is that good enough?"

Harald said that it was and so he became master of Mosul. An hour later, word came that fierce young Kamil had jumped to his death from the platform of the siege engine, rather than stand the dishonour of living in a city ruled by a Varanger. And two hours later a herald came in from General Maniakes commanding Harald to withdraw now and to hand over the governorship of Mosul to himself, so that the emperor in Byzantium should receive his rightful honours.

Harald told this messenger: "Go back to your master and inform him that the Varangers took this city and the Varangers shall hold it. Tell him to look for another city on behalf of the emperor. And, at the same time, ask him if his correct siege procedure would have done any better than our rough northern way."

At sundown Maniakes sent another herald, to tell Harald that if he did not surrender the city the Greeks would come in and fight them through every street and without mercy.

Harald was sitting with the emir, drinking iced fruit-juices, at this time. He lay back on the cushions with his mesh-shirt off and said, "Tell your master that I have no wish to fight Greeks. Tell him that half of what we plunder here shall be sent by escorted wagons along the Tigris valley and up to Trebizond. There the emperor's agents can see that it goes by ship to Byzantium. But if Greeks come storming in now it is likely that the emperor will lose the lot, because we of the Varangers are in no mood to be bullied any further."

That message must have been well delivered, because an hour later, from the high parapet of the citadel, the Varangers saw General Maniakes and all his host move away into the desert with banners flying, southwards, as though they meant to assail Bagdad itself.

Harald said to the emir, "You have seen more of life than I have, sir. Will you tell me if I answered General Maniakes correctly or not?"

The old man said sadly, "You are either a very wise man or a very great fool, Hardrada. Who am I to say which? A man must act as he thinks fit at any moment in his life. It is only later that he knows whether he acted as God wished him to act. All I can tell you is that if it is your wish to abandon your infidel ways and to accept Allah, then I will adopt you as my son in place of poor Kamil."

Harald said, "My dear brother Olaf was a great Christian, sir, and it would ill become me to betray his faith. Besides, if I were to be your son, how could I plunder Mosul and send the treasure I have promised to the emperor in Byzantium?"

The emir nodded his head. "If you argue always as sternly as this," he said, "you should make a very useful king one day, when Allah calls upon you to sit on a throne."

After that Harald and the emir became great friends. The Varangers, who were weary from their long march across the desert, welcomed the chance to live in houses for a while. So they stayed for over a year in Mosul and no doubt would have stayed longer but for a plague that swept the city during the following summer. Then they decided that it was better to be out in the open, where the winds could carry away disease from them, than shut in among alleys and courtyards where death could find them only too easily.

When they were about to leave the old emir sent for Harald and said, "You have behaved well during your time here. We Turks shall not forget the Varangers from this time on. It is the opinion of my greatest adviser that you are in every way the equal of the Turks."

Harald bowed and answered, "I have learned much, being with you, sir. And I would tell the emperor himself that there are as many good knights among the Turks as there are anywhere in the world that I have seen so far."

The emir waited a while, then he said, "If I may advise, from where I stand, on the topmost rung of the ladder towards Paradise, I would ask you to avoid this emperor of yours."

Harald smiled and asked, "You are a wise man, sir. You must have a good reason for saying that. What is it?"

Then the old man said, "I spoke with the Turcopole captain who once had dealings with you. He tells me that, from a Greek spy his men captured out in the desert, he finds that your General Maniakes is back in Byzantium and has charged you with high treason before the emperor."

Harald said, "That is no more than I expected. But I have dealt with Maniakes before and I shall deal with him again."

The emir looked away and said, "This time it will be different. Michael Catalactus has publicly pronounced the death sentence upon you, Harald."

Harald nodded and smiled. "That was to be expected," he said.

The emir gazed at him with interest. "You take it well," he said. "A Muslim would take it no better. But, my dear young man, you do not ask what manner of death is arranged for you."

Harald said, "Death is death, sir. I am only sorry that I sent that wagon-load of plunder to Catalactus now. I am afraid I have treated you badly and him too well."

But the emir waved his hand as though dismissing this, and said, "The form of your execution is this: that in the Hippodrome before all the people, they will first draw out your eyes, then chop off both your hands and, at the last, when they have had time to enjoy your punishment, they will tie you to four wild horses and let them drag you into pieces."

Harald said, "They call themselves the most civilized people in the world, sir. Well, I am sorry that I took anything from your treasury; but, if it helps to make amends, I will forego the half which I had planned to take for the Varangers. Will you pardon me for what I have done already?"

He fell to his knees before the old man and bowed his head. The emir could not speak for a time but at last he laid his hands on the Varanger's head and said, "With all my heart, my son. Now, will you not think again about staying here with me in Mosul? I would see that your life was as happy as I could make it. The folk here love and respect you. Great fame could come to you if you stayed."

Harald rose and gently placed his hand upon the emir's arm. "Father," he said, "you are the kindest man I have known since my dear brother Olaf died. If I could stay, I would; but I feel that I must seek my fame elsewhere than here. Besides, my folk are restless now and want to be away. But I shall always remember you with love."

The Turk felt inside a cupboard for his Koran so that Harald should not see the tears in his eyes. He said, "Then, if you must leave Mosul, Harald, go to Egypt; but do not go back to Byzantium, I implore you. I will give you letters to the caliph there, who is my friend."

Harald went to the window and gazed down into the square. He said at last, "After what you have told me, Father, if I did not return to settle accounts with Maniakes, I should never be able to call myself a man again."

19 · The Gathering Host

So Harald and the remaining Varangers went back towards Antioch. He had money from the emir with which he could redeem his ships in the harbour there, and many gifts besides, including what was said to be a fragment of the True Cross, set in silver and adorned with emeralds; three prayer rugs edged with designs which were, when read out, passages from the Koran; an ikon framed in silver-gilt, thought to have been left behind at Antioch after the battle of Yarmuk, when the Emperor Heraclius was so terribly mauled; and plentiful food supplies.

All this was carried in wagons loaned by the emir, who also sent a strong bodyguard to ride with the Varangers until they came clear of the desert.

It was a sad leave-taking but one which Harald had to make. The old man came to the gates of the city with him and in view of all the people took him in his arms and said, "When you have done what has to be done for honour's sake, come back, my son. This will always be your home."

Harald bowed his knee before the Muslim but did not reply.

The journey towards Aleppo was more pleasant than it had been coming the other way, for the weather was cooler, the food supplies were good, and there was not the same need to travel in heavy war gear. Though Harald lamented often that he had lost so many good men, one way and another, in that expedition.

But even this sadness lifted a little when, one bright morning, the wagon-train came upon the Turcopoles, sitting in perfect order, waiting for the Varangers. The captain said to Harald, "Sir, we have seen the error of our ways. Lead us back to Byzantium and we will take the oath again."

Harald took the man's hand and said, smiling grimly, "Yes, I will take you back, for it is likely that I might find a good use for you."

Then, only three days from Aleppo, the train caught up with a company of two hundred French and Italian foragers, many of them knights, who had come into Saracen land to make their fortunes but had found nothing but hardship and death in the dusty places they had visited. These men looked on Harald almost as their saviour and swore to obey him in all things if he would take them into his army.

He told them sternly, "I hope that you know what you are promising, for where we are going there are likely to be more kicks than halfpence. And many men who walk now on two legs will need a crutch for the rest of their lives, unless I am mistaken."

But they cried out that without his leadership they were no more than lost dogs in a foreign land. So at last he said, "Very well, my dogs from France and Italy, you are no longer lost—but you have taken upon yourselves a master who will use the whip if his whistle is not answered at the first blowing."

At Antioch the ships were waiting, though now with so many in his army Harald had fears that his vessels would be overloaded. But not one man who had vowed to serve him would stay behind. Wulf said, "Let them come, brother. It will not be the first time we have sailed with the water up to our knees."

And Haldor said, "Where we are going, the more swords at

our back the better; for I do not like this death they have arranged for you in the Hippodrome. And it is high time that these Greeks learned what it is to threaten the Varangers."

So the whole army sailed, cramped in their ships but happy to be on the move once more. During a spell of bad weather they put into port at Famagusta, and later rested up in Rhodes, since some of the ships needed caulking after their long stay at Antioch. The Turcopole captain wanted Harald to set a course to Athens so that they could see what sort of place that was, but he shook his head and said, "From here we shall go north among the islands, as straight as the ships will steer. I have business affairs in Byzantium which will not wait while you go sight-seeing."

This time the Aegean was a peaceful sea to sail in. Word went before the fleet that Harald was coming and so all the corsairs saw to it that they were somewhere else when he passed.

One of the Frenchmen said, "The rumours one hears of this sea! We were told that the place swarmed with cut-throats."

Eystein said starkly, "You must not believe all you hear."

Their food and drink supplies were running very low when they came within sight of the city. The Varangers cheered when they saw the great walls again and all the high buildings with Hagia Sophia standing proudly among them. Wulf said, "They may be laughing on the other side of their faces if this Maniakes is waiting for us at the harbour."

But all was quiet there and the army of Hardrada marched through the streets to the imperial palace without seeing a single Greek soldier. But when they came to the Forum of Constantine they saw rank upon rank of men waiting and leaning on their axes.

Gyric of Lichfield said grimly, "I thought it was too good to last. There must be over three hundred men there and though they are not enough to stop us, they are enough to spoil the looks of a few of us before we get through to the far side."

Eystein said to him, "You need not worry, Englishman. Your looks have already been spoiled."

Gyric said, "You speak in envy, sheep-islander. There are great queens who would say that I was a very proper man to look at."

Eystein rubbed his nose and answered, "Aye, no doubt, the sort of queens they have in Serkland, with bones through their noses."

Just then the leader of the axe-men who waited for them called out, "Is it Harald the Stern? Is it the King of Norway?"

And Haldor shouted back, "You have guessed right. Who else stands seven feet tall?"

Then the axe-men came running towards them, their weapons over their shoulders and laughing. Their leader called out, "We are the new company of Varangers, come down the great river while you were away. Thank God we have a leader from among our own folk at last."

Harald gazed hard at the man and said, "You are Thorgrim Skalaglam."

The young man stopped and said in amazement, "Why, how can you know me? You have never seen me before."

Then Harald said, "No, but I stood beside your father at the affair of Stiklestad and he took many blows that were meant for me. These things a man never forgets. You have his face, down to the wart beside your mouth. I am pleased to have you, Thorgrim Skalaglam, if you are half the war-man your father was."

Thorgrim took the leader's hand and said, "There have been no complaints—at least, not in my hearing."

So they all went to the palace then and Wulf whispered to Haldor, "If Maniakes still stays when he has seen what we bring, then he is the bravest general in the world."

Haldor whispered back, "Now, when Harald is emperor

here, in about ten minutes, what shall we set our hands to first? I think that we should pull down this stinking Hippodrome of theirs, for I am sick to the heart of what goes on there."

Harald heard this and said, "Are you two tired of life, to tempt the gods so with your forecasts? Be silent and keep your eyes open. There is many a bright morning that ends with a thunderstorm."

20 · The New General

But there was no thunderstorm that day. The palace courtyards were deserted and the Varangers went where they chose. Harald took fifty of the most experienced men with him and made his way to the imperial anteroom. There the Chamberlains, shaking on their wands, bowed before him and opened all doors without question.

The emperor, Michael Catalactus, looking much older and greyer, waited for him, dressed in all his finest and heaviest robes and wearing his great crown. Harald noticed that the man's hands were trembling and that he could hardly speak at first when the Varangers came laughing into the room.

Harald said, "In Saracen-land there was some rumour that I had been condemned to death, Michael."

The emperor struggled to find words, then he said, "My dear general, my dearest general." For a time he could say no more. So Harald said, "Do you mean to say that I am to be a general and not a corpse?"

The emperor laughed thinly and nodded his head. "Kneel before me in the sight of your men, and I will formally award you the generalship of all the Byzantine armies."

Harald said stoutly, "Nay, Michael. Speak the words straight, to my face, with me standing, and my men will understand just as well."

And this was what the emperor was forced to do. When he came to placing the general's gold chain about Hardrada's neck, he found it difficult, for the Norseman would not bend his head an inch. But at last it was done and then Harald said, "There are two chairs here and I am tired of standing. Let us sit down, Michael."

He sat down first, not waiting for the trembling emperor. And then he said, "There was a man called Maniakes. I think he was the general here, years ago. Where is he now?"

It took Michael long enough to reply. He said in a hoarse voice, "That Maniakes should never have offended you as he did. But, you understand, I was powerless to intervene, general."

Harald nodded and said, "It is a hard life being an emperor. Where is Maniakes now, I asked?"

Michael Catalactus said viciously, "When that coward heard you were coming back to talk to him, he went with his army overland to avoid you, in the direction of Sicily."

Harald said slowly, "Then when we have rested and have enjoyed the festivities that you no doubt have arranged for us, we too will go to Sicily and find out how this Maniakes is getting on."

The emperor nodded his head. His dark eyes flashed. "Yes, yes, general," he said viciously, "find him and bring him back in chains for judgement. Or, if you choose, put him to death on the spot where you find him. You have my authority to do this for now you are the Supreme Commander of the World."

Harald snorted and said, "To tell you the truth, Michael, I feel just as I always have felt—like a young fellow called Sigurdson."

When the Northmen had gone Michael Catalactus sent for

a nobleman who had made a great name for himself as a runner in the foot-races held at the Hippodrome, and said to him urgently, "Off with you now to the house beyond the Adrianople Gate where our true general is hiding, and tell him to go to Sicily without delay with a band of picked men. He will get out of the city in secret, disguised as a merchant if needs be, and will find loyal men in Sicily who will obey him. Tell him to enlist the Saracens on that island, for he will need all the troops he can lay hands on. And when Harald Hardrada arrives there, as he means to do for his revenge, tell our general to use any means in his power to put an end to this Northman. For, I swear by all the Saints, if this is not done soon then there will be a Norwegian sitting on the throne in Byzantium at last. Go now and report faithfully all I have said."

And while this young man was racing across the city by back streets to deliver his message, Harald and his chosen company established themselves in the small but rich palace placed at the general's disposal, just off the Forum of Theodosius and almost under the Aqueduct of Valens.

And that evening while they were sitting about and amusing themselves with story-telling and singing, a court Chamberlain came to Harald and said, "Lord, there is a lady to see you."

Harald said, "Then bring her in. Do not keep her waiting outside. We will make a place at the table for her."

The Chamberlain smiled shrewdly and said, "Lord, this lady commands that you see her in private."

Harald raised his eyebrows and said, "Commands, does she? Ah, well, whoever she is, we will let her command for the last time."

So he withdrew to a small room with no windows or peepholes, and there the lady came to him in a heavy purple robe, which she flung back to show that she was the Empress Zoë. Harald led her to a chair but did not kneel before her. She stared at him hard for a moment, then smiled bitterly and said,

"So you are still the proud White Bear of Norway, Harald?"

He said, "My name is Sigurdson and I am as I always was, lady. What do you want?"

She said, "Since you first came here you have risen high in the world, Harald. By my wishes you became a Varanger, then a captain of Varangers, and now a general of Byzantium."

He answered, "I hope that I shall give satisfaction, lady." His tone was sour because he always hated to be reminded of any debts. She touched him on the arm and said, "My lord, you will give even greater satisfaction if you will see sense at last and will accept the imperial crown of the Holy City."

He pretended to think of this for a while, then said slowly, "There is already an emperor, lady. What would he do, poison himself or go into a monastery?"

She tapped her foot with impatience on the tiled floor, then said sharply, "Whatever you wish, my lord. But if I might advise you, it is always safest to deprive any claimant to the throne of his sight, for then his powers are strictly limited. This is one of our ancient customs and it has never been known to fail. Do not frown, my lord, it can be done almost painlessly."

Harald gazed at her, deep in thought, his great hand upon his chin and his cold grey eyes set full on her. She lowered her head and said, "For a wild Northman, you are one of the gentlest men I have met. But make no mistake, Harald, this is a harsh world we live in and if a man is to gain the highest position in the world, he must be prepared to act with craft and strength."

Harald made his lips smile, and this was worse than his frowning before. Then he said, "Gracious lady, when such a proposal is made to him, a man has the right to consider a while before leaping out into the darkness."

She answered smiling, "It would not be you who leapt into the darkness, my love, but Michael Catalactus."

Harald could bear many things being said to him, but when this empress addressed him so tenderly he felt almost disgusted. He said as politely as he could, "Allow me until tomorrow. I will give you my answer then."

Now it was her turn to frown; but at last she accepted his words with as good a grace as she could and went from the little palace in her secret litter.

And when he was sure that she had gone, Harald took Wulf and Haldor with him and went to the suburbs where there were three religious houses for noblewomen. He enquired for Maria Anastasia Argyra at them all and found that she was in the third. At first the lady-in-waiting at the gate would not let him enter, but he began to rave and beat about so much with his sword-scabbard that, afraid he would destroy the statues and ikons, she let him in. But Wulf and Haldor had to stay in the courtyard to keep guard.

When Harald saw Maria Anastasia now he was dumbstruck. In the time he had been foraging among the Saracens she had grown to be almost as beautiful as his betrothed, Elizabeth of Novgorod. And though she was shut away in this house, she was allowed to dress as well as any princess in the world.

When she saw Harald's shyness, Maria said, "General, do not move from foot to foot like that. We are friends, are we not? I have prayed for you twice a day, ever since you sailed away from Byzantium. So I am your friend. But are you mine? You seem almost displeased with me."

Harald said, "My lady, I am quite the reverse. But I am a little put out to think that I once used to carry you on my shoulders pretending to be a horse."

Then Maria said most sincerely, "General, that was the happiest day of my life. On such a horse I would gallop away to the ends of the earth."

Harald said then, "Lady, I am a paid soldier and have much to do before my oath has run out. But, I declare, if your life is not happy here and you wish to change it, then when I return from work that must be done in Sicily, I will come to you again and ask how you feel about the world. And if you still tell me that you wish to be away from Byzantium, then I shall not blame you, for it is not a city I would want to spend my life in. And when I go from here in my ship, I promise to take you with me to wherever lies on the way north. There are courts at Kiev and at Novgorod where a great lady like yourself would be treated with all courtesy. And there I will take you if you wish to go, or may my right hand let fall the great axe in my moment of need."

Then, like a war horse, he knelt before her humbly in a way that the Empress Zoë had never known.

And when he had left that house, Maria Anastasia began to sing like a bird with joy. When the lady-in-waiting came in to see what had happened, she found the princess lying on the stone floor with her cheek pressed to the spot where the Varanger had knelt.

The next day, just after dawn, Harald sent Wulf to the imperial palace with this message: "The General thanks your Serene Majesty for the great honour you have offered him. He has thought much about it and must now confess that he feels himself unworthy. God made him to live in tents and ships, not in palaces."

When Wulf came back to the general's house, he reported that the empress had bitten her lip with rage and had then smashed three ancient vases upon the tiled floor before ripping the hem off her robe in fury.

"It is my advice, brother," he said to Harald, "that we get out of this city while we are able. I have never set eyes on a woman so demented."

Harald smiled and nodded. "We shall sail for Sicily by this evening," he said. "Our work here is over for the time being."

21 · Ill Luck

Harald left the palace Varangers in the care of the new captain, Thorgrim Skalaglam, and told him to keep a sharp eye on the Bulgar regiment. Then he set off with forty galleys and provisions enough to last his army for half a year.

It was not the best season for sea-travel, and westerly gales often forced the fleet against the many islands they journeyed among. Three weeks out, two of the galleys foundered south of Lesbos, and a week later, another ran aground and broke its back on Paros.

In all Harald lost a hundred men in those misfortunes. Eystein said to him, "I have begun to wonder whether there is some god or other down this way to whom we have not made the correct observances."

Harald said gruffly, "We are Christians in this army, are we not?"

But Wulf came in then and said, "Aye, we may be Christians, brother, but that doesn't mean to say that there are not other gods than ours. Eystein may well be right. The gods hereabouts may take it ill that we, who are mere visitors in their country, do not make offerings at the shrines."

Harald sent them both away and sat down to ponder this. And in the end he decided that it would be well enough to make the offering of an occasional sheep or, say, a bronze bracelet—provided that, at the same time, one kept one's right-hand forefingers crossed, or said a silent prayer to Saint Olaf.

Yet, though this became the practice aboard *Stallion,* when Wulf went ashore on Cythera, looking for a clear spring, an ill-natured adder bit his ankle and laid him in bed with a blue leg for a month.

A physician that they took on board at Taenarum, when Wulf's ravings were at their worst, recommended that the sick man's leg be cut off to stop the poison from spreading; but Haldor gave the man such a dark look that he thought of another remedy, which worked, though they were almost off Syracuse before Wulf could walk again without groaning.

But, bad as Wulf's luck was, another had worse.

When Harald had been gone a week the lady Theodora came to the house where Maria Anastasia was and went into her private cell unannounced.

"Now then, my lady," she said to the surprised girl, "your third cousin, Alexander Lascaris, has asked for your hand in marriage. He is a substantial man of forty-five and will give you a fine house and servants to keep it in order. He requires me to give him your answer this evening."

Maria Anastasia said, "I do not wish to marry anyone, aunt Theodora. At least, not for a while."

Theodora paced up and down the room, making her heavy silk skirts swish. Then she turned sharply and said, "If the big Norseman asked you, would you marry him?"

Maria, who had been brought up to speak the truth always, said, "If he were to ask me, yes. But he is away in Sicily, and there is no likelihood of that happening."

Theodora sat down heavily and fanned herself. Then she said, "Tell me, girl, if it is not too much to ask of you, why would you marry this grey-eyed Northman?"

Maria tried hard to picture him but could only see a great vague figure in a bearskin coat, with an iron helmet on his head and heavy plaits of hair hanging down on either side of it. She said, "Because he is a warrior and a hero, aunt Theodora."

Theodora was ever so long in answering now. Her eyes went narrow and she seemed to pinch her white nostrils in, then she said, "So, your cousin, Alexander Lascaris, is a coward, is he? The rich man who would give you a fine palace, three white horses, a gilded litter, and all the clothes and jewels you could load on to yourself—he is a coward, eh?"

Maria turned away. "I did not say that he was a coward, aunt Theodora," she said. "I only told you that Harald the Norseman is a hero."

Theodora rose and went towards the girl. "Tell me this," she said, "do you ever dream of this Norseman? Answer honestly or I shall know."

Maria lowered her eyes. "Every night, aunt Theodora," she said.

Theodora smiled almost kindly and placed her hand upon the girl's shoulder. "And tell me," she said, "do you ever dream of other people?"

Maria shook her head. "No, aunt, truthfully, I do not."

Then Theodora slapped her quite sharply on the cheek. The blow left a white mark in the shape of four fingers held close together. "So," she said, "you dream of this great bear from Norway but you never spare a thought for your good cousin, Alexander, who, to my knowledge, has sent you at least three crosses of silver and a rosary of amber."

Maria began to weep. "Dreams are not things one can help, aunt," she said. "Besides, it is not because of gifts that one may fall in love with a man."

Theodora said stiffly, "Now you are teaching me the nature of love; I, an old woman, and you, a mere girl who had never been outside the palace until she came to this house. Is it some devilish pride that consumes you, girl? Or do you wish to see how far you can drive me to send me to the madhouse?"

These things were beyond Maria. She said, "Please, aunt, do not make me answer all these questions. I am willing for someone else to decide if I am right in wishing to marry only the man I am in love with. Let us ask the Patriarch, aunt."

Theodora snorted. "The Patriarch!" she said. "Why, that old sheep does not know his right hand from his left. Have you not seen him, in Hagia Sophia, groping round on the wrong side for the chalice? And you would ask him to decide your life, you foolish creature!"

Maria fell to her knees. "Then let us ask the emperor himself," she said in desperation.

Now Theodora started back as though an adder had struck at her. "The emperor," she repeated. "Michael Catalactus the Great! Can you, from your infinite store of wisdom, gained inside two rooms of the palace, inform me how long that Arab will survive, now that his general Maniakes and his captain the Norse rogue have gone away? Can you, O wise one, tell me whether this Michael Catalactus will even be seeing the dawn that breaks tomorrow, much less deciding on a foolish girl's choice of a husband? Can you? Can you?"

Maria did not try to answer the old woman's fierce questioning but turned and ran from the oppressive room. And when she had gone, Theodora turned to a Bulgar guard who stood close behind her and said, "Follow that silly girl and give word that she must be trained in obedience still further. Her lessons so far have not been strict enough. From now on she is to wear a hair-shift and is to eat one meal a day, of goat cheese and black bread. Water shall be her only drink, and not too much of that. As for employment, when she is not scrubbing the floors of the churches under guard, she is to be given a hammer and is to work in the quarry of Saint Angelus, where they are breaking up stones for the new Hippodrome stables. She will work there each day from dawn to mid-day with a chain about her right ankle like any other felon. And, remember to pass on this part of my command—if anyone is misguided enough to speak to this girl, then his or her tongue shall be clipped. That is all, now go."

22 · The Three Breakings

Break one thing in the morning and before the day is out you will have broken three. It is better to get the breakings over straightway, said the Varangers; so, when you find that you have broken the first thing, smash two other objects of no value—and then you are free of the curse.

A mile off the new Syracuse mole just after dawn, Harald reached out for a cup of voyage-ale that Gyric offered him, but let it fall in his weariness and the cup broke on the deck. Gyric shook his head and said, "Now, captain, let me see you break two more cups before we go in to haven. Otherwise we may end the day with a pair of worse disasters. I have no wish to see the prow snapped off and the mast down."

Harald said, "What! Break two more of these cups? We are so much in need of cups as it is, we shall be drinking out of our cupped hands like dogs before long."

Wulf, lying on his straw pallet, laughed and said, "When you next see a dog drinking out of his cupped hands, call to me and let me know. It is a sight I should remember all my life."

Haldor said, "Their dogs in Norway have hands, didn't you know, Wulf? They are not like our poor creatures up in Iceland who have to make do with paws."

Eystein was alongside in *War Hawk* and wondered what the laughter was about. Haldor shouted across to him, "Hey, Baardson, what are the dogs like in Orkney? Do they have hands, can you remember?"

Eystein called back, "Aye, Snorreson, and feet. And when they grow to be seven foot tall, we trim their tails and send them off voyaging to Trondheim. Most of them get to be kings among the Norwegians. They are very quick-witted, our Orkney hounds."

Wulf said, "That is more than can be said for their masters, then."

So they went on joking and laughing stupidly until they forgot what started it all. Nevertheless, there were two more things to be broken that day.

Now the eastern shore of Sicily was in their view. Away to the right hand they saw the grim and towering fire-mountain with snow lying on its upper slopes. Before them they saw a dozen rivers, like silver threads, rushing down the burnt rocks towards the sea.

Here and there sulphurous yellow smoke rose from low hutments among the stones, and beyond them, up the further ridges, ranks of dark-foliaged pines stood like waiting sentries, glowering down. The land had a grim and forbidding face, as though it warned all travellers to stay away from its shores.

Haldor said, "Sheep would get few pickings here. I can see but small grazing land, and that is as burnt as tinder."

Harald answered him: "We have not sailed so far to raise sheep, brother. Sheep will be the last thing in my mind when I come within a sword's reach of Maniakes."

Haldor replied, "In Iceland even the greatest warmen spare a thought for their sheep and their hay harvest."

Harald said, "Aye, and they like to go out fishing in the sea, too. But I never heard that these things filled their heads when they were out searching for an enemy. I never heard that when Kari was sniffing out the men who burned old Njal he spoke overmuch about sheep and hay and fish. The way I heard it, Kari was more concerned about that sword-blade of his, that got softened in the fire at the barn that night."

Wulf said, "Kari was a man in a thousand. After God made him, He broke the mould."

Then they had to stop their talking for the water between the two forks of the harbour-moles jolted them about as though they sailed on top of a boiling cauldron. It took Harald and Eystein in their two longships all their strength to keep the steerboards straight and the vessels from turning turtle.

And just when they were running through the gap, with the rest of the fleet strung out well behind them, Eystein shouted across, "What is that big thing I can see lying behind the crowded smacks in the middle of the harbour-shell? Is it a house on legs?"

Harald was too busy at that time to look where Eystein was pointing, but suddenly as they came safely through the gap, missing the nearside grey wall by less than a cable-length, there was a great whirring in the air and a stone came in a wide arc towards them, humming like a nest of giant hornets. Harald swung hard on the steerboard, but *Stallion* lay in a water-race that would not let the longship move a point from course. The heavy rock struck the masthead and brought half of the ash-pole down, crashing over the side and tangling the deck with sail and rigging.

Harald said, "I do not need to answer you now, Baardson. That house on legs is a catapult, as you can see."

Then the two longships did their best to swing about and go back between the moles and into the open water to safety. But *Stallion* would not answer to the board, though the Varangers had chopped away rigging and sail now, but lay wallowing in the water like a lame thing.

Eystein had got *War Hawk* half-way about and was shouting at the rowers to bend on their oars when a second rock came groaning through the air and stove in the strakes just below the shields on his steerboard side. The rowers on that side were flung on top of one another in a heap, though not a man was hurt.

Harald said starkly, "Well, there are the two breakages that

Gyric warned us to expect. It is a good thing to know the worst, brothers."

Haldor said, "While you were wrestling with the helm, they have put two stout chains across the gap. We can't get out, and the rest of the fleet can't get in to help us. So perhaps we haven't seen the worst yet."

Harald gave up struggling and sat down on the deck to hone his sword-blade. He said, "What can't be cured must be endured. We have run like flies into the middle of the spider's web, but we can still sting him a little before he makes a meal of us, brothers."

As he spoke two long galleys, black-painted and low in the water, streaked out at them one on either flank, like sea-snakes. They bristled with lances and on the forward deck of each was positioned a small fire-thrower, strung back in readiness for the cast. The men in these black sea-snakes wore white turbans and cloaks over their iron gear. Harald said, "Well, at least it is not the Greek who has caught us so neatly. We have that to be thankful for."

Gyric said, "When we are burned down to the water line and standing in the sea, remind me to be thankful again, Harald. I can already feel ingratitude creeping over me."

Harald laughed and said, "You worry too much, Mercian. This sort of thing is happening all the time, up and down the world."

Gyric answered, "I know that, friend; but somehow I always feel happier when it is happening to someone else."

Just then the foremost sea-snake, which lay less than a long bowshot from *Stallion,* drew up a little and a blue-robed man in the prow called across to them, "Are you Greeks or Normans?"

Harald put the leather trumpet to his lips and answered, "Neither. We are Varangers out of Byzantium, looking for Maniakes. This is a private affair and is the business only of Harald Sigurdson and his henchmen."

The man in the blue robe called back, "Stand well forward so that I can see if you are Harald Sigurdson."

This Harald did, holding himself up very straight and letting his great cloak billow out behind him to give him his full size.

And after a while the man in the blue robe said, "I can see who you are now. I am the Emir of Syracuse and no friend of Maniakes. What do you wish to do—be burned out of the sea, or come ashore as friends to the city?"

Harald shouted back, "What sort of answer do you usually get to that question?"

Then the man in blue laughed down his speaking-horn and said, "Very well, Sigurdson, we will tow you into haven as friends. After sundown, when we are sure of your good intentions, I will have the chains taken down and the rest of your fleet can come in behind you."

Wulf said from his bed, "I am glad it has turned out so. I could not have done myself justice, as I feel now, if they had come aboard for a tussle."

Haldor said, "This emir seems a reasonable enough fellow. Perhaps we can get him to have you made a little cart with two wheels and a pair of handles. Then I can push you into the battle-line when we meet Maniakes."

Wulf nodded and said, "That is a good idea, brother. But see that it is well padded. I feel as sore as though I had been thrashed, lying on this hard deck so long. I hope they have soft beds in Syracuse."

23 · The Emir and Hauteville

Wulf got his wish. The beds in the emir's palace were the softest he had ever lain in. And the food and drink were the best the Varangers had tasted since they sailed out of Byzantium.

The Emir Bouid was a pale-faced merry man who had studied languages and medicine at the great school in Cordoba before he took to arms; so he could speak and jest with any of the Varangers in their own tongues, but what was best, he had salves and potions which soon had Wulf skipping about on his poisoned leg as though it was a new one.

As they all sat on cushions by the brazier in his courtyard, Bouid said to Harald, "There is one thing that puzzles me about you northfolk; you are the best in the world at giving wounds, and the worst at mending them. Why is this?"

Harald said, "We usually leave it to the women, this wound-healing. They have their own remedies that are passed down from mother to daughter."

Bouid answered smiling, "Yes, I have heard of some of these remedies. When I was a student a young doctor from Paris told me about the roast toad that your women grind to a powder as medicine, and about your tinctures of earthworms and confections of wood-lice. He also mentioned the mould that you scrape off the bark of damp trees to put into a wound and then cover it over with a spider's web. I cannot see how such treatment could do other than kill a wounded man."

Haldor said, "Think what you like, Emir, but I can tell you that an uncle of mine lost the end of his nose in a night ambush up at Knafahills. He had the good sense to bring the piece home with him after the fighting, and my grandmother stuck it back on, with a paste of snails. It got to be the best-known nose in Iceland. It could smell out an enemy five miles away."

Wulf said slyly, "But you should tell the emir the full story. The old lady could not see very well and she put it on upside down. Men sailed from as far away as Dublin to see this nose afterwards."

The emir laughed at this story and said, "If I had fellows like you to stay with me in Sicily always, I should be the merriest man alive."

Harald said, "I have not noticed that you wept overmuch about the palace, Bouid."

The emir said, "That is because I weep secretly into my sleeve, Harald. A man like myself who has studied the Stoics does not display his grief."

Wulf said, "What do you weep for? Is it because your Prophet forbade you to drink wine?"

Bouid answered, "No, not that, Icelander. He was a stern man, surely, but a very human man. He knew that rules were made to be broken from time to time. Shall I send for another jar of wine so that you may see?"

Wulf said, "Please do, Emir. But when it comes, I shall see that you touch none of it, breaking the rules on our behalf. I shall drink it myself."

The emir said, "Such selfishness is most unChristian, as I understand your Prophet's teachings. We must share and share alike, Viking."

So Bouid sent for more wine and then Harald asked him: "Why do you say you are unhappy, brother? Your folk have been on this island for five lifetimes of a man; you have green plants growing in this desert, and lemons to make drinks from. You even have snow whenever you need it, in winter or summer, from the great mountain, to cool your wine. What makes you sad?"

Bouid answered, "We were once a great people, Sigurdson, and we shall be so again; but in the meantime we have fallen on bad times. We cannot agree with one another. From Gades to Bagdad we quarrel and quarrel. And each time we quarrel we weaken ourselves by bringing in mercenary soldiers of other faiths to fight for us."

Gyric laughed and said, "It is no bad thing to be brought in, if one is by trade a mercenary soldier, emir. I would fight for the King of India if he offered me more than the King of Africa."

Bouid nodded, then said gently, "Of course, of course. A knight must look to his trade, that is understood. But, my friend, it is sometimes disturbing when a king of one's own faith brings in pagans to fight fellow-Muslims. This is happening now with the King of Tunis, who calls himself my overlord, but fetches in the Norman foragers to bring me to heel if I do not leap to obey his most stupid commands."

Harald was enjoying the wine. He said pleasantly, "Life is a very difficult book to read, Bouid. Each page seems to have so many hidden meanings, and every word has so many various shades."

Wulf said, "You never told us you could read, Harald! When did you learn, on the way down from Byzantium?"

Harald put on a stark look and said, "The trouble with Icelanders is that they will try to be merry at a greater man's expense."

Then Wulf and Haldor made a great show of looking round the courtyard to see where such a great man might be. Harald wagged his long finger at them and said, "There will come a time when you two will be sorry you ever taunted me. When I sit on the throne-chair in Norway, one of the first things I shall do is to gather a great fleet round me and sail to Iceland to teach it its manners."

The emir smiled slowly. He said, "Your family have always

been sailing to teach someone their manners, Harald. When I was in Zaragoza once I met an old monk from Essex in England who told me of a kinsman of yours, Anlaf, he called him, who took the ships over to beat sense into the heads of the English."

Harald clenched his jaws and did not answer. Wulf nudged him and said, "Come now, Sigurdson, your kinsman Olaf won the day at Maldon. You have no need to be ashamed of him, even if he was a heathen at the time. A man has to learn some time, and he hadn't learned then."

The emir nodded and smiled. He said, "This old monk told me how the battle went—with the Danes outnumbering the English—and how, at the end, the English began to sing in their shield-ring. It was a wonderful warrior-song he told me:

Thought shall be the harder, heart the keener,
Courage the greater, as our strength faileth.
Here lies our leader in the dust of his greatness;
Who leaves him now, damned be for ever.
We who are with him shall not leave this battle,
But lie at his side, in the dust with our leader.

That is the sort of song my people used to sing when we first started out from Arabia."

Harald snorted. "Maybe," he said. "We all learn better as we get older."

The emir poured another cup of wine for Harald and put into it a spoonful of honey and a spoonful of ice. He said, "I wonder if that is true, friend? I wonder if we all lose some of our great honest virtues when we get to be more knowing, more crafty, more clever—but less wise?"

Harald was about to answer him in strong fashion when a trumpet screamed outside and the door was flung open. Standing there and smiling down at them was a young man of perhaps twenty, who wore black armour and a fox's russet brush in place of a plume in his helmet. His face was raw-boned and red and his hair was a bleached sandy colour. His long sword scraped the tiles of the floor when he walked.

He said above their heads, "I am the youngest of the Hautevilles. Which is the man they call Hardrada?"

Harald rose from beside the brazier and said, "I am Harald Sigurdson, young man. Do you wish to speak with me?"

The young knight shook his head. "No," he said. "The message that Maniakes ordered me to deliver was not sent in words. It is this."

Then as he spoke, he suddenly reached out and struck Harald hard across the face with his iron-meshed glove. The wine-cup fell from Harald's hand and he drew back a pace, the blood showing on his grazed cheek.

Wulf called to him, "Shall I pass you the sword, Harald? Or am I to use mine?"

But Harald said, "No, he is a herald and is delivering a message. We must follow the correct procedure in such matters or the story-tellers will report ill of us."

So he walked up to the young knight, who stood there still smiling, with the fox's brush bobbing about on his helmet. And Harald said to him pleasantly, "When you go back to Maniakes of Byzantium, will you do me the favour of passing on my reply?"

Hauteville the knight nodded and said, "Certainly, Varanger."

No one except Gyric of Lichfield saw the two blows struck. And he had good cause to observe how they felt for he had once felt their weight himself.

And while the emir's servants were reviving the knight with cups of iced wine, Harald fingered the fox's brush and said, "This is well enough as a sort of jest, but should not be worn seriously by a warrior."

So he threw it into the fire and watched it crackle and burn.

Then he drew the knight's sword and gazed at it. "This is too long a toy," he said. "This young fellow will surely trip over it one day if it is not shortened for him."

So he put the sword across his knee and broke a foot off the end of it. Then he slipped the two pieces back into the scabbard.

And when Hauteville was fully awake again, Harald stroked his cheek and said, "Such a young fellow to come carrying so heavy a message. Well, my lad, do your best to take my own greeting back to the Greek. And good luck go with you."

Hauteville staggered up, felt for his fox's brush and could not find it. Then he swayed to the door and leaned on the lintel a while to get his bearings. While he was there he said to Harald, "I am young now, Hardrada, but I shall grow. And when we meet again you shall have reason to know that I am bigger than I was."

Harald bowed to him and said, "You are always welcome, my boy. And if you do not feel strong enough for such discussions in the future, I beg you to bring your family with you."

Hauteville said gravely then, "Have no fear, Norseman, I shall bring my family. And when you see them you will feel very lonely, for I have eight brothers and twenty cousins."

Harald said, "Then our meeting will be a sad day for their fathers with so many funerals to pay for, little one."

And when the knight had gone, the emir said, "Whether you did well or ill, I cannot tell you, Harald. But now you have offended the most powerful clan of Normans that the world has known. They have already frightened the Pope out of his wits and even have the Byzantine emperor in their grasp."

Harald said, "I am not so easily frightened, my friend. And whoever grasps me must have a hand three times the size of any that God has so far given to man."

Then he went back to his wine-cup by the glowing brazier.

24 · Gyric's Call

A few days later Harald was walking in the olive fields with Emir Bouid when suddenly Gyric came running towards them and waving at them to stop. Harald laughed at him and said, "What is it? Are the ships on fire in the harbour?"

Gyric went up to Harald and touched him on the chest and arms and then said, "Thanks be to God."

Harald said, "I will agree to that any day of the week and twice on Sundays; but why come running through the olives on such a warm day to tell me you are thankful?"

Gyric began to sway his head and shuffle his feet sheepishly, which was a very funny sight since he was so big and awkward in all his movements. At last he said, "Did I ever tell you that my grandmother on my father's side was Black Torfi the witch who lived in a sandstone cave at Wednesbury in the shire of Stafford?"

Harald shook his head. "No," he answered, "but I am always glad to hear of great folk, wherever they come from."

The mild-tempered emir regarded Gyric with an amused smile on his pale face, so Gyric said to the Muslim, "My grandmother Black Torfi once shook her stick at the wooden spire on Wednesbury church and it fell to the ground. That was because the priest there would not spare space for Odin in his devotions. At Cleobury in Shropshire the same thing happened; but this time she only carried her small stick with her and it lacked the full force to bring down the spire there. Instead, it twisted like a corkscrew, as you can see to this day."

The emir said, "That lady would have been useful in certain

campaigns I have been on. Her stick would have succeeded where my siege-engines failed, it seems."

Then Gyric took Harald by the sleeve and said, "Listen well to this." And he threw back his head and shrieked, "Hroar—Hroar—hek—kek—kek! Hroar—Hroar—hek—kek—kek!"

As he did this a flock of birds flew, terrified, out of the grass and rose into the sky chittering.

Harald said, "Most interesting, Gyric. But what has it to do with me?"

Gyric said, "I want you to do it, too."

At first Harald would not do this, but the emir was so amused, he said, "Do it, to please Gyric, Norseman, and I will try to do it with you."

So the two did it until they could send up birds wherever they stood. And then Harald said, "Come, now, Gyric. A joke's a joke. What is this you have had us doing the last hour?"

Gyric said, "It is the warning cry of the goshawk, captain. It is the sound he makes when he is furious with an enemy and wants to get his beak and claws into him."

Harald said, "This is a most interesting day; I have learned how to bring a church steeple down, and how to yell like a hunting-bird. What more could a man want in this world? Against such learning, gold is nothing."

Gyric sulked in the olive grove for a while, then he turned to Harald and said, "Very well, laugh at me if you wish, and see if I care. A man like you is so big in the bone that he outgrows his brains. You are the biggest viking-booby I ever had the mischance to meet. And if you ever sit on the throne in England, I shall make it quite clear to my fellow-Englishmen what sort of king they have got."

The emir said, "Something has put you out, friend Gyric. Tell me, what is it? I am never likely to be King of England, so you have no need to glower at me."

So Gyric told him. He said, "As I lay asleep by the well in the outer courtyard, emir, I seemed to see Harald lying in a stone pit, with blood all over him and his clothes torn away. And there were a dozen men above him, poking down at him with spears and laughing at his plight."

Harald wiped his face for it was a very warm day, and said, "That was a bad dream. But warmen are always having bad dreams, especially before battles, and in any case you eat and drink so much that I am not surprised at such a dream."

Gyric said, "Not surprised, hey? Well, let me tell you this, Harald Not-so-surprised, that all of these men with spears wore the brush of a fox in their helmets. And, worst of all, as you lay down there, you had no sword. You could not defend yourself. Now are you surprised, big Norsehead?"

Harald's face went very white then. He leaned against a tree as though with shock and said, "You did right to tell me, brother. These Hautevilles caught me without a sword, eh? And took vengeance on me in a stone pit?"

Suddenly he turned to the emir and said, "Are there such stone pits on this island, friend?"

Bouid nodded his head. "They are everywhere," he answered. "You will find them in the big farms and the castles, where they are used for storing grain through the winter."

Harald said, "I must remember to keep away from granaries then, and must not be caught without my sword, is that it, Gyric?"

Gyric said, "I have not told you all. At the end of my dream one of them jumped down to you with an axe in his hand. It was the young one who came to the palace with the message. I will not tell you what he did then."

Harald smiled and patted the man on the shoulder. "Thank you, brother," he said, "I do not really want to know. I can guess well enough."

Gyric took him by the arm and spoke seriously to him.

"Then," he said, "I woke up with a start and said a prayer for you. And while I was kneeling there by the well, it seemed to me that my old grandmother, Black Torfi, was whispering to me out of the grave. And she was saying: 'You must teach the Norseman the warning cry of the goshawk, grandson. See that he learns it well, for it could save his life.' So I promised her I would do as she advised and I ran all the way here to do it—and small thanks have I had for my trouble."

Harald turned to the Englishman and said, "I am sorry, brother, with all my heart. If ever I am so dim-witted again when you come to tell me something of importance, fetch me a clout that knocks some sense into my thick skull. Will you do that for me?"

Gyric said, "I wish I could promise that, Norseman, but I have come to love you like a son, and if the devil himself had me, I couldn't bring myself to lay a finger on you, dim-witted or not."

The emir put his arms round both of them as they walked on through the grove, and he said, "I admire the way you northfolk speak with one another. In the old days when my people were finding themselves and striking out at all who stood in their way, the captains spoke to the kings, and the soldiers to the captains, in the way you folk speak. They spoke as straight as the arrow flies, which is the way that men should speak to each other. But now those good days are over, and in the name of courtesy men speak with one another in such riddles that it is hard to know what they mean half the time. Let me advise you, see that you always speak as you do now, and one day your peoples will grow to be truly great. For straight speech is a sign of strength, of honesty of purpose, and no people can stay great without these qualities."

But Harald was not listening. He was practising the warning-call of the goshawk again and making swarms of birds rise from the fields and irrigation ditches every time. Gyric walked behind him, nodding his head and grinning hugely now, his awful dream almost forgotten.

25 · The Caliph's Pact

On the same day that Harald learned how to call like a goshawk, Maria Anastasia Argyra was working in the quarry of Saint Angelus on her hands and knees among the stone when a dark shadow fell before her. She looked up, drawing her hair from before her eyes, and saw that it was the Curopalates who looked after the private affairs of the emperor in the palace. He was a very tall thin man and was dressed very splendidly indeed. He looked down at the princess with distaste and said, "Your hands and feet are very dirty and your nails are broken. I see that your hair is thick with stone dust."

Maria Anastasia did not answer him. She felt her eyes were full of tears and did not wish to humble herself by weeping before this man.

So he said, "This dress they have given you to wear, it is not very becoming for one like you. It is more like rough striped sackcloth than anything else. It must be very trying to the skin. And that length of rusty chain which you wear as a girdle, surely you do not like that?"

Maria clenched her teeth and said, "No, I do not like it. But I do not like the perfume you are wearing either."

The Curopalates was offended at this. He raised his eyebrows and began to sniff rather delicately. Then he said in a sharp voice, "When I visit such places as this, I use such a scent to protect my nostrils from plagues and pestilences. No doubt you are by now used to the smells of prisons and quarries, but I, I am glad to say, am still an admirer of cleanliness and decency."

Maria put down her hammer and stood up with some effort because of the shackles about her ankle. She put her hands on her hips and said to him quite calmly now, "I too am an admirer of cleanliness and decency, Curopalates; but if I had to choose between the sort of people I have met in the quarry and the sort that mince about the imperial palace with their silver wands, then I would choose my friends down here."

The official waited until she had finished, smiling with mockery all the time, then he said, "Between ourselves, it is my opinion that Byzantium will be well rid of you, child. I do not think that your ancestor Constantine Argyrus the Macedonian would have approved of you. In fact, with your crude habits and appearance, you seem to me to take after your other forefather, Basil Bulgaroctonus, the Slayer of Bulgarians! His hands were red like yours as I remember him in my youth. He always looked more like a peasant than an emperor."

Maria said evenly, "If you have come here merely to insult me, my lord, then consider that your work has been well done and that you are now at liberty to go back to the palace and make your report. For I have no doubt that as with every other trivial thing in this place, a lengthy report will have to be drawn up by the scribes and then entered into the court records in at least three places."

The Curopalates nodded and smiled. "Something like that," he said. "It is the custom and always has been the custom. So who are we to change the habits of our greatest of cities?"

Maria Anastasia said angrily, "I sometimes wish that the Turks would come into the Golden Horn and sweep all this ancient custom and habit away. It lies on us like a cold dead hand from the past and I find it sickening."

The official bowed and said, "I will have such a note made in the records, my lady. It might be helpful for the emperor to know your considered opinion on the matter."

Maria said, "The emperor is not interested in any opinion that I hold, my lord. Nor can you frighten me by threatening to tell him what I have said."

The Curopalates stroked his long nose and smiled. He said, "In the present circumstances I think that the emperor might be very influenced by your opinions, my lady. Moreover, in those circumstances, the emperor would do anything rather than harm you, whatever you chose to say on any matter."

Maria wondered why he spoke in this way; his next words answered her. He said, "Life does not stand still, my lady, however much it might seem to do so for one working here in such depressing conditions day after day. Let me tell you something which you may not know: long before you were born the Caliph of Cairo, whose name was Hakim, went mad and ordered the destruction of the Church of the Holy Sepulchre in Jerusalem. After that he proclaimed himself to be God and so his subjects very properly got rid of him."

Maria said, "I have heard all this many times before. You did not have to come so far on a hot day to tell it to me again, sir."

But the Curopalates smiled and said, "Have patience, lady. There is a new part to the story which even you have not yet heard. His Most Serene Majesty, Michael Catalactus, has recently made a pact with the present Egyptian caliph and has been given permission to rebuild the church over the grave of Jesus Christ. Is that not good news? Do you not rejoice that once more our pilgrims will be able to travel to Jerusalem under imperial protection to say their prayers in a church rebuilt by Greeks?"

Maria said, "Of course. There is no need to ask. But I can see by your face that you have more to tell me. What is it?"

The official nodded and said quietly, "Do you think that pacts are made as easily as all that, child? Do you not know that there are often small conditions made between great princes when a pact goes forward?"

Maria now felt her legs trembling as though they would let her down. She said, "These conditions—do they affect me?"

The Curopalates nodded. He said, "You and certain other ladies of Byzantium are to go to Egypt at the caliph's request."

Then Maria flung herself down on the pile of stones she had been working at and began to weep bitterly.

The official raised his eyebrows again pityingly and said, "It is not every young woman who is permitted such an opportunity to travel in these times. You have the satisfaction of knowing that the emperor approves of your journey, and that the caliph will look after you as befits a princess of the imperial house. Who knows, child, if you are amenable to Saracen ways, one day you might rise to be an important person in the world. He has many sons, and to have a Macedonian princess once more in power in Egypt would be a great advantage to Byzantium. No doubt, with your great learning, you will recall that Cleopatra was also a Greek of sorts. Our fame and heritage are ancient and wide-flung. When you have had time to think of what I say, you will bless the moment I walked into this stone quarry. Now I will leave you."

He went away, but Maria did not raise her head to watch him go, picking his way carefully with his long wand. Instead, she wept and wept until her tears ran over the stones she had hammered earlier, and two African slaves came from their own heaps of rubble to stare down at her in wonder. She kept crying out, "Harald, oh, Harald Hardrada." But the two Africans knew no language but their own, so shook their heads at last and left her to her solitary weeping.

26 The Hunt Begins

Word came to Bouid from one of his spies that General Maniakes had set himself up in the fortress of Catania, almost in the shadow of the great fire-mountain, and was daily gathering more and more men about him, including many wandering Norman knights.

When Harald heard this he said, "There is no time like the present, friend. Your army and mine together could put an end to this Greek."

But Bouid stared down at the mosaic tiles and said at last, "That was my dream, to ride with you, brother. But now I hear that the King of Tunis has sworn to burn me out of Syracuse and is getting ready to send a fleet against me. His harbour lies only a hundred miles from here and, with the right wind, he could be knocking on my door before Catania fell."

Harald slapped him on the back. "That is no reason for making such a long face, brother," he said. "Such things could happen to any general. You must stay here and beat back the Tunisians. I will go with the Varangers and give short shrift to Maniakes on my own. After all, it is my quarrel and not yours."

But Bouid looked hardly any more pleased at this. He said, "The fortress there is a very ancient one, with walls that have grown thicker in every century. It would need many strong siege-engines to bring down such walls and as I am placed at the moment I scarcely dare let my catapults out of my sight."

Again Harald laughed. "Friend," he said, "even if you dared, I have no men who could work them. We Varangers travel light and fight light. We are not engineers. So set your heart at rest, beat off the Tunisians, and we will put our longswords to the work in hand and come back to you as soon as we have the head of Maniakes on a pole to show you. Is that well?"

Bouid nodded sadly. "It is as well as can be expected, brother," he said. And so, the following day, the Varangers set out towards Catania, carrying little with them in their journey up the coast of Sicily.

They arrived at twilight on the second day and set up camp near the river Simeto, meaning to make their first assault just before dawn on the morrow. But when they came in sight of the castle Wulf blew through his cheeks and said, "We have as much chance of getting into that stone beehive as an Iceland dog has of dancing an Irish jig."

But Gyric of Lichfield shook his head and said, "I have certainly not come as far as this just to look at the place and then go home. I shall walk round the walls and see what I can see. Then perhaps I will teach you Norsemen something you did not know before."

Eystein Baardson came up just then and said laughing, "Watch how you go, Lichfield. They have three hundred archers on top of that wall, waiting for someone like you to step within range."

Gyric gave him a hard look and answered, "When I get an arrow in my jacket, that will be the first time, friend."

The Varangers watched him go and saw the bowmen on the walls making ready; but Gyric passed out of sight beyond the walls without a bolt being loosed off at him, although the men on the walls called out all the time, inviting him to step a little closer.

Gyric was away all day and by sunset some of the Varangers had begun to make wagers on him, laying odds against his return. But just after the red sun fell behind the Hybla mountains, Gyric came back into camp with a grim smile on his face, footsore and very thirsty.

Haldor went to meet him and said, "I see three holes in the skirt of your mesh-shirt. They look very much like arrow-slits to me, friend."

Gyric shrugged his shoulders and said, "Aye, that is what they look like. In my great thinking about this fortress, I happened to turn my blind eye towards the walls three times. It is at such time that one may walk against briar thorns and rip one's shirt."

Harald called out, "Less of this bragging, Gyric. Come and tell us what you have learned."

So Gyric sat by the fire and drank three cups of ale before he would say another word. And when he did, he said, "Well, I have prowled right round this place and have stood on a little hillock that gives a good view of the roofs."

Wulf said, "That is most interesting, friend. And were the tiles of pretty colours?"

Gyric said starkly, "There are no tiles. All the roofs are thatched, dearest of comrades."

Then Harald said, "No doubt your grandmother the witch would know what to make of that, Gyric, but as a plain soldier I must confess that you have baffled me."

Gyric cut himself a piece of beef and placed it on a thick slab of barley bread and began to munch. "All that walking has given me a great appetite," he said. "I could eat a horse."

Wulf said then, "If you do not speak some sense very soon we shall find a horse and keep you to your word, if we have to ram it down your stupid throat."

Then Gyric laughed and answered, "Very well, little vikings, if your own frozen brains won't give you the answer, then mine must. I have been watching the roofs of Catania all day while you have been lying in the sun boasting about your old victories. And what I have noticed is that this place is not a beehive, but more like a home for birds."

Wulf began to say something then, but Harald waved to him to be silent, and Gyric went on: "I have never seen so many birds at one time in my life before. They fly in and out of the thatch in all places."

Then there was a long silence, for the Varangers had all clustered round the fire to hear Gyric's words, and now they looked at one another in bewilderment.

So Gyric turned towards them and said, "You are a brisk set of fellows, my friends. Let each one of you who knows how to catch a bird hold up his right hand."

Then, amid much laughter, five men put up their hands and Gyric said, "Very well, my friends, then waste no more time but get about your trade and fetch in as many birds as you can before night comes down on us too heavily."

So the men went away, with nets and cloaks and anything else they needed; and when they had gone, Gyric said to the others, "Now all of you scout round and bring back to me thin twigs of resinous wood, and any jars of oil or cauldrons of pitch you can lay your thieving hands on."

Then he went back to eating more meat and drinking more ale. And when he had satisfied his hunger and thirst, Harald said to him, "I have been in a few battles in my time, but never in one where the fighting-men were set on to catch birds."

Gyric looked at him wickedly and said, "We learn something every day, if we keep our eyes and ears open, do we not, Harald?"

He would say no more. But later, when the men came back with the netted birds all fluttering and squawking, and the others had laid down their heap of small dry twigs, Gyric said, "Now I want the men with the nimblest fingers to take twine and to tie the sticks on to the birds' legs and tails, put a light to the wood, and send these little creatures back home."

Harald shook his great head and went away to sit down beside Eystein. He said to the old sailorman, "I do not know who is the bigger fool, Gyric for thinking up such a scheme, or myself for letting him do it. But, what is certain, by tomorrow my name will be the one that sets all men laughing from coast to coast throughout Sicily."

But even as he was talking he saw a rush of fire across the sky, moving towards Catania. And shortly he saw a roof burst into flame and heard a great deal of shouting from the high walls.

And while he was still staring in bewilderment at this, another house took fire, then another and then another. And soon the whole of the fortress was blazing from the roofs downwards.

Then Gyric strolled over to the brazier where Harald stood and said, "We may not get into this place, captain; but those who are already in will be most anxious to get out before an hour has passed."

And he was right. In much less than an hour the great gates swung open and townsfolk came streaming out beyond the walls. From where the Varangers waited, their swords drawn, they could see the stones of the fortress growing white and chalk-like and could hear some of them splitting up with a loud noise.

Then Gyric said smiling, "Are we ready to move in, Harald?"

And that is what they began to do, each man keeping his eyes open for General Maniakes. But when they were a bow-shot from the walls, a party of men-at-arms came out holding their swords by the points to show that they were of a peaceful mind. They were led by a Greek lieutenant whom the Varangers knew well and who flung himself on his knees before Harald and said, "My lord, such as is left of this place, we surrender to you."

Harald glared down at the man and said, "It is not this

burnt-out heap of rubble that I have come for, but your General Maniakes. Tell him to come out and stand before me."

The young lieutenant rose and spread his hands. He said, "My gracious lord, that is not possible. When he saw that the flames could not be put out, the general escaped from the far postern in a beggar's cloak and riding a fast horse. I beg you, be merciful to the townspeople here, they have no quarrel with you."

Harald said grimly, "I have never punished townsfolk yet for what the soldiery have done. But I shall change my habits this night unless you tell me faithfully where Maniakes has gone. By dawn the folk of Catania shall learn what it is to lock their doors against a Norseman."

Then the lieutenant wrung his hands and said at last, "I have no alternative. Though I betray my general, I must tell you where he is, for I am a Christian and could not go to my grave with the lives of so many innocent citizens on my conscience."

Wulf took out his sword and held it at the lieutenant's throat. He said, "Let us have the news we want, not a sermon. We are not in Hagia Sophia now, friend."

The Icelander's face was so red and fierce and bristling that the Greek fell on his knees once more and clasped his hands. "Have pity, my lord," he said, "and I will say a prayer for you every night of my life from now on."

Wulf said starkly, "Save your breath, youth; I would rather know where Maniakes has gone."

"Then," said the Greek, "I must tell you. Our general has gone across the mountains to Licata, where the Tunisians are gathering and have promised to side with him."

"'Good," said Wulf, kicking the lieutenant over, "then we will also go to Licata. Why should this Maniakes have all the amusement in this world?"

27 · The Tunnel at Licata

But the journey over the mountains to Licata was not the pleasure that Wulf had said it would be. There was much hard climbing to do, under a harsh sun, and up sharp rocks that tore through shoe-leather and left feet raw and bleeding. Besides, since the Varangers travelled light to make good speed, they carried small provision with them and, since there were few houses and no villages on the upper slopes of the mountains, after the third day Harald's men began to wonder if they had been wise to follow Maniakes after all.

When at last they reached the ridge and looked down on distant Licata, the Varangers were more like parched scare-crows than warriors. Few of them could walk without groaning and all of them limped. If Maniakes could have met them then, on the mountain-top, he would have found but slight difficulty in putting an end to their hunting.

Then, by good luck, the weather changed suddenly. Heavy black clouds settled low over the mountains and without warning thunder and lightning burst forth, and then the rain came down as though it would never stop. The Varangers stood in the downpour, letting themselves get soaked to the bone, even lapping up the water as it flowed down their sun-scorched faces. Some of them began to dance like bears and to give thanks to Thor for sending his lightning; but Harald quickly put a stop to this by reminding them that they were Christians and not heathens any longer.

And when the storm had worn itself out and the men had rested, they began their long march down the far hill-slope towards Licata. Now in a pine-wood they were lucky once again, for they found a herd of swine picking about under the low boughs. And that night the wood was heavy with the smell of roasting pork.

Before dawn the next day they struck a tributary of the river Salso and followed it down towards the coast. The water had chiselled such a deep gully through the rocks in this part that the whole army could march onwards without being seen. Haldor was in high glee at this and called out to Harald, "I feel in my bones that this time we shall be in great luck. I would wager my front teeth with any man that this time we shall have good cause to rejoice. What do you say, Gyric?"

But Gyric was in one of his dark moods and answered, "No one wants your front teeth, friend. They have teeth of their own, so keep them where they belong for chewing your meat with. As for rejoicing, you should know well enough that it ill becomes any warman to rejoice before his foes lie stark at his feet. I shall say no more."

Wulf said, "And that is just as well, if you are going to croak at us like a Lichfield raven."

After that the Varangers went down towards the coast in silence. Once Harald climbed to the lip of the gully and looked to the sea. Then he cried out, "The Tunisians have indeed come. Their galleys lie off-shore in great droves like sheep. It is as well that Bouid stayed where he was, with his famous siege engines, at Syracuse. He is a wise commander, that much I will say for him."

Eystein snorted and said shortly, "I hope we shall say the same of you by the time we have taken Licata, brother."

But when the Varangers had had a chance of looking at that castle, they began to wonder if there was any commander who could take it by storm, without the help of engines. Its walls were high and had broad platforms jutting out on every side, from which flaming asphalt and pitch could be poured down on to any attacker. Moreover, there was no cover for three bowshots all round the defences, so that a siege-party would have to move over an open space to get close to the walls. Since the Varangers carried with them no sows or defence-engines, they stood in danger of losing half their number at least in trying to breach this place.

Gyric looked up at it wryly from the cover of the gully and said, "I see that their roofs are tiled here. We cannot use our little friends the birds this time."

So the Varangers sat down beside the sheltered river and there was a great gloom over them all. But Haldor was still in high spirits, and he went off to spy out the land. When he came back, he said to Harald, "There is one place where this river loops round and runs within fifty paces of a corner tower of the castle, brother."

Harald said shortly, "What is in your mind, then? Have you some new way of fighting wars too?"

Haldor slapped him on the shoulder and said, "Now, look, brother, a man does not have to be a great scholar to dig a hole in the ground, does he?"

Harald said, "So this time we must burrow like moles and come up from under the floor inside Licata, is that it?"

Haldor nodded. He said, "I have examined the earth down here and it is soft. Though we have no entrenching tools, our swords and spears would pick away the earth. We could approach this tunnel-making in a long line, each man passing back the earth we dig out in cloaks. Then the last man could fling the soil into the river and it would float away and leave us a clear entrance."

Just then Wulf came back from foraging and said, "I have even a better thing to tell you. God has done half the work for us already. There is a little underground stream that comes out into the river. If we enlarged the tunnel it makes, I have the feeling that it would lead us up into the castle well-shaft."

Now Harald said, "You both speak good sense. Forgive me

if I was short with you. I am often a dull dog. So now, since the luck seems to be with us, let us do nothing to drive it away. We must light no fires from now on; we must not even talk in whispers to one another. There will be no eating and drinking until we break up through the floor into this castle. Is that understood?"

All the Varangers nodded that they understood their captain's orders, and then they filed up the gully to the place where the little stream flowed out. And there they began to dig, as silently as ghosts.

Though the men worked in relays it was no easy labour. They had two consolations, though: first that the path into the fortress was already marked for them, and secondly that their spears were of the broad-bladed Varangian sort and not the thin-pointed lances which the Bulgar regiment carried.

As the day wore on and the bright sunshine outside turned to dusk, the Varangers drew nearer and nearer to the well-shaft. And at last, when they had been picking away for twelve hours, Harald whispered to Haldor, "I am standing knee-deep in cool water and all about me I can feel stones, set in a circle above my head. Above me, I think I see chinks of light, as though torches are shining up there, beyond the well-cover. What should we do now, brother?"

Haldor whispered back softly, "We have no mounting-ladders but it seems to me that this shaft is only an arm's width broad. So we must go singly, each man pressing his back against one side and his feet against the other and inching his body upwards."

Harald said, "I am not in favour of that. If the top man fell, as he might do easily enough on this slippery stonework, then he would take the others down with him and we should all be trapped in the tunnel for them to do with us as they pleased."

Wulf pushed up towards them and whispered, "You two

chatter like the washerwomen of Bergen round their well. Let someone who knows put an end to this talk. Now listen to me: you, Harald, being the heaviest man in the world, must stand at the bottom forming a stirrup with your two hands locked. Haldor must then mount on to your hands and then on to your shoulders and stand with his back against the wall. I shall then climb up both of you with my axe in my hand, and from Haldor's shoulders I shall easily reach the well-cover. This I shall hack across with three skilful strokes in my usual manner, then I shall jump inside the room and draw Haldor up after me. The other men will follow on up while he and I hold back the Tunisians. Is that clear?"

Harald said glumly, "And I am to stand down here in the water while all the army climb on to my back? Is that the part for a captain to play?"

Wulf said, "That's your fault for being so tall."

Haldor said, "If you think I am going second into this castle, Wulf, then you must think again. Unless I go in first, with the luck upon me as I feel it now, I shall not go in at all. Then you will have that to explain when we get back home to Iceland—how you deprived your closest friend of his greatest moment."

Wulf said sullenly, "Very well, since I can hear tears in your voice, little one, you shall go up first. But I tell you this, if we meet with disaster because of your childishness, then I will vow to kick you every inch of the way back to Reykjavik."

So Haldor began to smile again and pushed Harald hard against the wall and made him stand firm. Then Wulf went up on to the captain's shoulders and at last Haldor clambered up both of them with his sword between his teeth.

His heart was so light, at being first of the host, that his throat wanted to sing like a blackbird. His feet went up and up, over hands and shoulders, until he thought that, with a little practice, he could learn to climb a castle wall. Oh, he thought, how good it is to be a Varanger! Is there any trade like this in the whole wide world? Tell me, but is there?

Then his head struck the wooden well-cover and, pressing hard with one hand to balance himself against the slippery wall, he took the sword from between his clenched jaws and struck upward with a mighty clout. He had judged the grain of the wood aright and the cover split back in two halves, leaving Haldor blinking in the bright torchlight for a second.

And that second of blindness was enough to bring his downfall. For at the very lip of the well stood a dark-faced Tunisian guard with a moon-shaped battle-axe. As the viking swung himself up into the chamber, this axe flailed out in a wide sweep, and Haldor found himself swept aside with the blow's force, one side of his head sadly hurt.

Wulf heard his high cry of pain and leapt like a lynx from Harald's broad shoulders into the room. Seeing his comrade lying so broken, he roared with fury and took the Saracen below the helmet flaps with a savage thrust. The man fell backwards and in falling knocked down the flaring torch and put the place in darkness.

Down below in the tunnel the Varangers began to cry out with battlelust. Now they made no pretence at silence but swarmed upwards into the dark chamber. One of them had the sense to strike flint on steel and light the torch again, and then as they assembled in this room they saw that it was not a feast hall but a food larder and that its great inner door was secured with five iron bolts.

Four of the Varangers drew up Harald on the end of their knotted sword-belts. He was the last of the host to enter Licata and the saddest.

He gazed down at Haldor who lay senseless and wept without shame, like a young girl. He said, "Our poor brother offered us his front teeth earlier today. But now he lacks any teeth at all to offer. In return for this blow Maniakes shall know what it is like to eat porridge for the rest of his dark days."

And then there was a great knocking on the door and a stern voice called out, "I am the King of Tunisia's emir. Who are you within there?"

Harald shouted back in rage, "I am Sigurdson, the Hardrada of Norway, the Bear of the North. I have come for Maniakes the Greek, and after I have taken him, I shall crunch up all others I can find in my jaws."

As he spoke the froth gathered at his lips so thickly that Eystein and Gyric were afraid for his reason. But the Tunisian emir on the other side of the door said quite calmly, "Maniakes is no friend of ours. He is not here, I can assure you. If he were, it would give me pleasure to watch you crunching him up as you say."

Now all the Varangers crowded into that dim food larder began to shout, "Where is Maniakes? Where is Maniakes?" And to beat their swords and axes against anything that would ring out and make a noise.

And at last the emir answered, "Where should he be but in Palermo? That is where his Norman allies are gathering like vultures. Why do you not go there and leave us to our own affairs? We have work enough to do in Sicily, without fighting your battles for you."

Now Haldor was starting to moan with the pain that had come to him when his wound had lost its numbness, and Harald sat on the floor cradling his comrade's head and rocking backwards and forwards in grief.

He waited a while, then said, "I am in such a mind, Saracen, to destroy all the world for what has happened to my friend today."

And the Tunisian answered evenly, "What else did you expect to happen, when you break into a defended castle? Have you not grown out of your dream yet, Sigurdson? Do you still think that war-making is a sweet pleasure, then? Have you not seen your comrades lying stark before? Then you must have met slight opposition, my friend."

Gyric could see that this sort of talk would lead nowhere, so he called through the heavy door, "Look, Tunisian, we hold your food supplies and inside three days we could starve you out of Licata. Then where would you be?"

And the emir answered, "So, if we are to starve then we will see that you do not profit by your possession. We will fire the whole castle and sit outside the walls to hear you howling as you roast."

So it was that in the end Eystein, who still kept his head clear, arranged that the Varangers should come out unharmed and that the emir's physician should do what he could for Haldor.

But despite his skill this was little enough. The doctor, who was a quietly spoken Berber with hair as russet as any Frank's, said with pity, "It is a sin to ruin God's handiwork in such a trade as you folk follow. You rush like fire across the earth, you northfolk, foraging and destroying, giving ghastly wounds and taking them for mere plunder. We physicians spend our lives trying to repair the damage you do; yet once it is repaired you are off again trying your hardest to give us more work."

Eystein and Gyric felt ashamed to hear him say this. But Harald stayed in a dark corner, brooding silently, and holding Haldor's cold hand.

Two young girls who had been trained in medicine at Basra helped the Saracen to deal with Haldor. After binding his wounds with salves and herbs, they made a mask of doe-skin which they hoped might help to give shape back to his features. They did not cut eyeholes in this mask because the Berber physician thought it was most unlikely that Haldor would ever see again.

And that was how the Varangers tunnelled into Licata to find Maniakes. It was two months later before Haldor was able to be moved from that castle again; and when he went out it was not on his own two feet but in a litter like an old man.

Yet his spirit was as strong as ever. When Wulf asked him if he wished to travel with the host to seek the Greek general in Palermo, he nodded so violently that the physician forbade them to speak to him any more that day.

28 · The Other Brothers

At length, as they came to those fertile lowlands near Palermo that men call the Golden Shell, Harald was in such a dour frame of spirit that few men dared to talk with him. Even before they had left Licata, Eystein had seen this coming on and had sent a secret messenger to Bouid in Syracuse to tell him of the Tunisian garrison on the coast. And, since Harald seemed to have lost interest in what they would do after they had caught Maniakes, Eystein had also despatched a company of Varangers by night to Syracuse, sufficient in number to bring the fleet round to lie off the Palermo Roads until they were needed. Harald did not miss them. Men said that Haldor's wound had so upset him that he would not have missed his left hand if it had been taken from him in the night.

But his right hand was another matter. When he was not clasping Haldor's hand with it, he was clenching it and striking out at anything that stood in his way; and each time he struck, he cried out, "Maniakes! Maniakes!" and then gritted his teeth so frightfully that those closest to him expected him to grind them to dust before long.

Wulf was little better. He would stand and stare at Haldor for an hour at a stretch, and then run away into the woods to weep and to slash out with his axe at the trees as though they were Greeks.

As for Haldor, he lay for a long while in a dazed sleep, as though he did not wish to drag himself back to life. The great hardship was that his jaws were so broken he could neither eat nor drink. But as soon as he dared, the Berber physician inserted the narrow tip of a cow's horn into an incision which he made just below Haldor's jaw and through this his friends poured milk sweetened with wild honey, or sometimes stout red wine, and even fine-flavoured meat broth. And in this way the life stayed with him.

Then one day, when the host looked down on Palermo, Haldor suddenly shuffled upright in his bed and reached for his sword. Gyric, who was sitting with him, was afraid lest the Icelander had come to the end of his tether and wished to make away with himself as the old Romans used to do, by falling on the blade. But Haldor signalled to him that all was well; and when he had the sword in his hand he felt its balance as though he had never held a weapon in his life before.

Then all at once he stood up, threw back his head, and struck out at the ashpole of the tent. The blade sheared through it like a knife through cheese, and then the canvas flapped down on Haldor and Gyric, sweeping them to the ground.

Varangers came running up to see what had happened, and when Gyric told them, they knew that this was the best sort of news and crowded round Haldor cheering him and laughing. And when he signed to them to cut away the doeskin mask from his face they found a small keen knife and obeyed him, though the features that glared out at them were not those of any man they had ever seen before.

But all men observed that Haldor's eyes were open and clear, so there was that much to be thankful for. And as the vikings gathered round him, nodding and smiling at him, he pointed to his lips and then they saw that he was able to open his mouth a little way. They bent towards him listening, and he said in a faint whisper, "The axe has not yet reached the anvil that could lay me down."

Wulf burst into tears at this and flung himself on the ground. Eystein ran at a fresh ale-cask and knocked the bung out so that the liquid spouted all over the place. Gyric took up a new linen shirt and ripped it into small pieces in his joy. Then he ran to Harald's tent and told him what had happened.

For a while the Varanger glared as though his senses had left him. Then he rose and took Gyric by the hands and clasped him so hard that the Englishman cried out, half-way between glee and agony.

Then, with the tears streaming down his face, and his great sword over his right shoulder, and holding it by the point, Harald stumbled away from the encampment into the wood to be alone.

He found a small glade surrounded by pine trees with a little stream running through it among the light green mosses, and there he knelt and prayed as best he could, in thanks for his friend's deliverance.

And when he had run out of all the words he knew, he rose and roared out wordlessly, his head thrown back. Then he flung his sword from him across the glade and saw it stick bolt upright and a foot deep in a little green hummock beyond the stream.

Then all at once he knew how hungry and thirsty he was. And he recalled that no food or drink had passed his lips for three days while he had sat beside his wounded friend. So he shambled towards that little stream and fell to his hands and knees and lapped at the clear water like a dog.

And even as he lapped his eyes caught a strange shimmering in the water, a shadow that passed as fast as a lightning streak and then was gone. And at the same time Harald heard something hiss behind him through the air, and as by instinct he drew aside. A sharp-pointed lance plunged viciously into the turf beside him where his head had been an instant before. It was a Bulgar lance.

So Harald swung round, still on his knees, and there before him grinning stood the young Hauteville he had knocked to the ground at Syracuse. Harald gazed past the knight's stiff mask of a face at the eight men who rose from the bushes behind him, their swords in their hands and the foxes' brushes bobbing in their helmets. He said, "I see you have brought your brothers with you, Hauteville."

The young man said, "It is not every day that the foxes run a hound to earth. We like to make a good job of these affairs."

Harald said, "You will see that I have no sword, Hauteville."

The young man nodded. "I see," he said. "That will make it the more entertaining for us."

Now a great fury rose in Harald's heart towards this young knight who stood calmly drawing his long dagger from his belt. Staring the youth fixedly in the eye and speaking as evenly as he could, Harald said, "I have seen prettier pig-stickers than that in my time." Then, even as he was speaking, he grasped a handful of mud from beside the stream and flung it into Hauteville's face. The dagger swept out in a bright flash, but Harald stepped inside it and chopped down harshly with his right hand. A great shout of anger went up as the young knight fell face downwards to the ground. Harald bellowed like a penned bull and stamped the youth's face into the marshy turf.

Then the Hautevilles were rushing at him like furies, almost slashing one another to be first at the kill. As blade clashed on blade and brother jostled with brother savagely, Harald caught sight of a pine branch above him and leaped upwards with all his strength. The point of one sword passed through the skirt of his tunic as he went. The flat of another caught him on the thigh but did not cut.

And then he sat on the bough, out of sword's reach, laughing down at them and gasping for breath. He said, "If you will have the goodness to pass my sword up to me, I will show you something else before I go."

They glared up at him, raw-boned as wolves, their grey eyes starting and their teeth showing. And the most furious of all was the youngest who now rose from the marsh with mud up to his eyes. Harald called down to him, "See that you wash your face before you sit down to meat tonight, my boy. Now throw me up my sword and I will come down and visit you lads."

The youngest Hauteville shrieked out in fury then like a mewed hawk, snatched up the Bulgar lance and thrust with it at Harald's legs. But it failed to reach him by at least a foot, so Harald said, "That is no way to bring a bear down out of a tree, my boy. Take aim and throw the spear and let us see what sort of marksman you are."

But one of the elder Hautevilles cried out, "Do not cast it, brother. These vikings have the trick of catching spears in mid-flight and turning them back on the sender. Let us not be hasty; we have all time before us. We will take this vengeance at our leisure."

So some of them sat down by the stream, and others leaned on trees and watched. Then the youngest Hauteville bent and took up a handful of pebbles from the waterside and began to fling them at Harald. Some of them flew past his head but others struck him sharply on the arms and body.

Harald had the good fortune to catch one of them and to bounce it off the youth's right shoulder, sending him away howling with pain.

Then the Varanger said sternly, "Let that be a lesson to you not to fight like peasants and thralls. If you are men enough to wear swords, then be men enough to use swords."

But these words were his undoing, for while he spoke he did not notice one of the older and stronger men bending to pick up a large stone. It was this one which struck him beside the right temple and toppled him from the bough.

Yet even so his senses did not leave him utterly. He clutched out as he fell and so hung by both hands from the pine-bough. But now his plight was desperate for the smallest of the Normans could have reached him with the sword.

But this was not their way. They could see well enough that if Harald tried to climb back on to the swaying branch his great weight would snap it short; and if he let go, he would fall to the ground at their feet. So they took their time and at last they fetched the youngest Hauteville and put the lance back into his hand. "Now take your vengeance, brother," said the eldest. "He cannot throw another stone at you."

As he hung there helplessly, Harald thought how stupid such an end was. He had always assumed that he would die in the usual manner, with his back set against the standard, or holding on firmly to the sinking prow. But to be spiked while dangling from a pine-bough was no sort of death to be recalled in a song. He was thinking how curious life was—which gave him back an old friend and took his own life, all in one afternoon—when a great sharp pain came up under his left arm and he bit through his lip rather than howl out.

Down below him he heard the young Hauteville laugh grimly and the brothers congratulating him for his thrust. Then Harald knew that his left hand had fallen from its hold on the branch and was hanging down helplessly by his side. And as he waited for the next thrust, for want of something better to do, he called out at the top of what voice was left him: "Hroar—Hroar—hek—kek—kek! Hroar—Hroar—hek—kek—kek!"

At first he heard them laughing below, then all at once there was a great rushing sound and a fierce trampling of the brushwood round the glade. Harald looked through the sweat that streamed down his face and saw Gyric flailing his great Danish axe and the Hautevilles falling before him like mown wheat or taking to their heels. And close beside Gyric stood Wulf hissing like a fiend with every blow of his long sword. And just behind him, old Haldor, tottering like a crippled bear but swiping out so terribly and grinning with his fearful new face so horribly that the Normans faded before him like wood-smoke.

And then Harald fell from the bough, all his strength gone, and lay beside the little hummock where his sword still stuck up like a headstone on a grave.

The last spark of his senses had left him now so he was spared the grief of seeing Gyric fall beside him, a cloth-yard arrow deeply embedded between his shoulder-blades.

He was spared the grief of hearing poor Haldor crying out wordlessly at the death of one of his dearest comrades.

29 · The Great Darkness

A great darkness hung over the Varanger encampment. Some of the oldest rovers there said that they had never known such times and prayed for Harald to recover so that they could shake the dust of Sicily from their feet since, they swore, it was an accursed island and had always been so. No one since Minos the Great had prospered there. No tree came to its full growth in such parched soil, they said. The gods were angry with such a place, or why else should they set a fire-mountain on it to threaten all men?

A party of the youngest vikings who had seen little service before this voyage, and who had not been hammered into an iron-hearted host, lost courage at these words and slipped away towards the north-east coast, taking their chance on finding shipping to carry them to Denmark, and another leader to follow.

Harald's wound was so deep and angry, his fever so great, that at last Eystein forgot all pride and sent to the Berber physician of Licata for aid. The man came over the mountains on a mule and leading an ass behind him laden with a medicine chest. But when he had examined the wound and had probed deeply into it, he shook his head sadly and said, "This is beyond my curing. If I had been here when you brought him in, I might have done something; but the weapon which made this hole must have been unclean, for now a poison has spread through this man's whole body. The best we can do for him is to make his last hours comfortable ones."

So they washed Harald and put fresh clothing on him and propped him up on feather-cushions beside a brazier on which the doctor burned aromatic woods and spices. And by this bed they set a cup of spiced wine on a low table in case he should wake and feel thirsty.

In the next tent Haldor lay, sick from his exertions in the wood and barely conscious. Wulf knelt beside him, holding his hand and saying, again and again, "Forgive me, forgive me, brother. I should have gone in first."

Eystein saw that Gyric had a high funeral pyre of all the various woods they could find about the Golden Shell. They poured on to this great heap oil and wine and milk that they could ill afford, having no supplies but what they foraged for by night. And when they had dressed him in his war-shirt and helmet, and had laid sword, buckler and spear beside him, they put fire to the mound.

A fresh wind blew up from the sea, fanning the flames into a fierce blaze and sending up showers of sparks into the evening air. And when the fire was at its height a great grey bird came swooping down, then paused and hovered a while over the pyre before it turned and set course again for the north, crying out sadly.

Eystein said to the man beside him, "Did you hear what that bird cried, friend?"

The viking nodded. "Aye," he said, "it was old Gyric's call, and that bird was a goshawk, master."

Eystein said, "I thought my ears did not deceive me, friend."

Then he went back to Harald's tent and found the Varanger sitting up and staring towards the open door-flap. And when Eystein went towards him, Harald said quite clearly, "I have just heard Gyric calling me to come to him, Eystein. He was sending out the goshawk cry. I must go to his aid."

He struggled to rise then but Eystein caught him as he toppled sideways and said, "Lie still, captain. I have just come from Gyric's side and I swear to you that he was not crying out then."

Then Harald fought hard to see Eystein clearly, and when his eyes were steadily fixed on him he said, "You swear that Gyric is in no danger?"

Eystein clenched his fist and said, "I swear by Thor's hammer, captain, or may I never thrive again. Nothing will hurt Gyric."

The Berber heard this and when Harald had lain back on his pillows whispered, "You did the only thing a man could do for his friend."

Many times that night Harald roused and asked hoarsely if Gyric was safe, and each time Eystein nodded and smiled. And at length the Varanger fell into a calm sleep with his hands folded on his breast.

The Berber came into the tent and said, "I must leave you now, for my duty lies with the King of Tunis. If the God your captain prays to is kind to him, He will let Harald float away from this harsh world while he is sleeping so peacefully."

Eystein had barely returned from escorting the Berber safely from the encampment when a tall old man, wearing a black cloak and carrying his round helmet below his left arm, came up from Palermo among the Varangers. The wind whipped his close-cut white hair about his head and reddened his thin, sun-burnt face; yet there seemed to be something in this man's features and bearing which were strangely familiar to Eystein, who stood and waited for him to speak.

And when the old man was five paces from the sea-rover, he stopped and flung open his cloak to show that he wore no hauberk beneath it. Then in a firm, quiet voice he said, "My name is Hauteville, and four of my sons lie dead."

Eystein said gravely, "I know. I was there. Have you come for blood-money or vengeance?"

The old man answered, "Neither. My little foxes should have known better than to tree the Bear of Norway. It was their misfortune and I thank God that I still have five sons left."

Eystein said, "Keep them under lock and key or you will have five less to thank God for."

Then the Varanger saw that tears were coursing down the old man's cheeks, although his face was as firm-set as ever. At last Hauteville said, "Sir, in all my life I have never bent the knee to any man, and until this moment these eyes had never shed a tear. But now my heart is so laden with shame and sadness that I beg leave to go on my knees before the Hardrada and to ask his pardon for the wrong that has been done."

Many Norsemen had clustered round the old knight and had heard what he said. They cried out, "Let the old one have his wish, Eystein. Let him pay homage to the Hardrada, it is his due."

And so the famous Norman was led to Harald's bedside and,

seeing what a ruin his sons had made of the great hero, he fell to his knees and put his lips to the hem of Harald's robe.

As he did so, the Norseman's eyelids flickered and he moved his head and looked down sleepily on Hauteville. "I know who you are," he said. "Do you wear the fox's brush in your helmet too?"

But old Hauteville did not answer this. Instead, he bowed still lower and said, "My lord, I am here to ask your pardon."

And Harald, struggling hard against sleep, replied, "You shall have it and willingly—in return for the head of the Greek, Maniakes, who began this quarrel which has cost the blood of too many good men."

Hauteville rose then and said gently, "That price is beyond my power to pay, my lord. We have already driven the Greek from Palermo and he is out of our reach now. We could not tolerate his pride and arrogance."

Harald whispered harshly, "If you were following him, as I am, where would you look, Hauteville?"

The Norman said grimly, "I would search in Crete, for that is where the merchant-ship he sailed in was bound."

Harald said, "Then that is where we will go. I have come too far now to be cheated of my rights."

Hauteville stared round the tent at the faces of the sea-rovers, then he said to Eystein, "Your captain must not be moved. Or, at least, no further than the castle I hold in Palermo. There he might lie safely, with priests and physicians to watch him until the end."

Now Harald spoke almost as clearly as they had ever heard him and said, "When I enter that castle, Hauteville, it will be walking, on my own feet, not carried on men's shoulders. I cannot use my sword lying down."

Hauteville bowed towards him stiffly, then backed to the tent-flap and said to Eystein, "This is the greatest man living in the world today, sea-rover. When his spirit passes from him, see that he has a ship-burning that will do him justice. He is the last of the vikings."

Then he turned and left the tent so that the great Norseman should not see a Norman weeping. But Harald had already fallen back into sleep.

30 · The Darkness Lifts

About this time a wet season began on the island and before long the Varangers found themselves penned in their tents with the rain lashing hour after hour at the canvas and the light dimmed by storm-clouds. The ground between the lines was sodden and a man could sink to the waist if he stepped from the rocky path. To make things worse, by now almost half of the rovers suffered from sickness and could keep no food or drink down.

At last one of the men came to Eystein and said, "Shipmaster, if we stay here we shall all die, there are no two ways about it. Each night we see the flares burning on our vessels off-shore, where they wait for us. Yet we lie here on mouldy straw, wet to the skin, and many of us starving. We are as brave as any men, Eystein, but now we face an enemy that sword and axe cannot touch. Let us go, master, while we still have the strength to drag our limbs down to the shore."

Eystein said, "Helge, if any other man had said this to me, I should have struck him down. You have lost a brother and a cousin on this island, so you have the right to speak. But, know this, that if we move the Hardrada, he will die."

Helge answered, "I do not speak for myself, shipmaster, but for two hundred comrades. If it were to be the exchange of one life for another, I would gladly give mine so that Harald should live on a while; but I doubt whether even the Bear of Norway values himself as two hundred men."

Eystein said sharply, "That is for him to say. We will ask him."

Harald was lolling against a cask, his eyes open but vacant, his great fingers playing idly with a strand of wool. When they stood before him he smiled at them briefly, then looked down.

Eystein said, "Brother, Helge tells me the men are sick."

Harald waited long before replying, then he said, "Poor lads, they are only alive when the prow is bucking before them. They are like me, they stifle in anything but salt air."

Then Helge went forward and fell on his knees before Hardrada. "Lord," he said, "the men say you are going to die."

Eystein put his hand out to stop the man, but suddenly Harald frowned most fiercely at his friend. Then he said, "Aye, lad, that is what they say."

So Helge said, "Then, lord, where would you rather be, here on the cushions, or on your thong-bed in *Stallion's* after-cabin?"

Harald swayed then as though he would fall, but he suddenly recollected himself and whispered through his clenched teeth, "Carry me there, I beg you."

Helge dared to take Hardrada's hand and clasp it tightly. "Master," he said, "you shall go aboard your longship tonight if Eystein has my head for it tomorrow."

As he spoke he turned and looked up at his sea-captain defiantly. But Eystein was nodding sadly as though he knew that this was the way it would turn out in the end.

And so at dusk the Varangers lit brushwood flares up the coast, away from Palermo, and fetched in the fleet. It was a long affair in managing, for the wood was damp with the rain; and when they came to carry Harald in a litter the bearers must go as softly as night-thieves so as not to jolt him on the uneven ground.

They moved off like ghosts, taking only their weapons and war gear. They left their tents to flap deserted in the rain, or to be torn to shreds by the winds that came up from the sea. And soon after midnight they were aboard and standing off-shore, waiting to set a course to Crete.

No ships came out of Palermo to hinder them, though it was plain to the watchers on the castle-towers that the Varangers were withdrawing in a sorry state and were in no condition to defend themselves against sudden ambush.

And in the small hours when a north-easterly breeze from Taranto filled their sails for the voyage round about the island, Harald sent for Helge and said to him, "Do the men feel better now, friend?"

Helge told him that they did and that they blessed his name. Then Harald said, "When you go back to them, tell them that I bless their name too, for already the darkness is lifting from me. My fever is less and the pain of my wound is not what it was. Salt is the best medicine and the sea is the best mother. Feel how she rocks us in our cradle now, Helge."

The man nodded to humour him but Harald shook his head a little and said, "Do not treat me like a fool, Helge. It is my body that is hurt, not my brain. Now tell me this, is Gyric dead?"

Helge nodded his head. "Yes, master," he said. "They were afraid to tell you before."

Harald said slowly, "I have been waiting for them to tell me, Helge. They should not be so tender-minded. Gyric is well-pleased where he is. He has come to me three times in a dream to tell me so. He has told me other things, too; that Haldor will be well again one day, but that I shall never be the king in England."

Helge smiled and said, "I dreamed once that I was flying like a bird, but when I got up from bed and tried to do it again I fell into the fiord and had to be dragged out with a boathook. Dreams do not always speak the truth."

Harald said, "So you cannot fly, eh? I should have thought that a brisk young fellow like you could fly, Helge. Yes, I should have thought that."

Helge looked sharply at the Varanger, but Harald was asleep now in that rocking longship, and for the first time since Licata there was peace upon his face.

31 · The Dress-fitting

Maria Anastasia Argyra stood in the imperial chamber while six sewing-women bustled round her with rolls of silk net, cloth of gold, and brocade so heavy and encrusted that it stood out as stiffly as a board—and was just as tedious to wear.

With her face so pale, her hair combed down to her shoulders so straight, and her enormous skirt flaring out from under her arms to the mosaic floor, Maria looked more like a doll than a girl.

The Empress Zoë lay back on a Turkish couch, watching everything and holding a small fan of green peacock feathers in her jewelled hand. From time to time she moved this fan slowly, sending waves of incense wafting across the dim room, like a child idly playing.

"Keep still, child," she said sharply to Maria. "The woman may be a clumsy animal for sticking a pin in you, but a princess of the Macedonian royal house should be above noticing such trivialities."

Maria had been standing in the stuffy room all afternoon and, with such a weight of clothing upon her, she felt ready to drop.

The empress said thoughtfully, "We will have you made a tall diadem of silver set with pearls for that dress. Pearls will look well with the black brocade. There shall be a high collar of seed-pearls to go with it. We must cover your neck, it has grown so skinny recently. Your arms too; we will put bracelets along them and then the caliph will not notice how like a skeleton you are. And please stand still when I speak to you, girl. Do you think I enjoy spending all this money on a skeleton that will totter and sway on its feet at every word? Now look up a little. Yes, your face is far too thin. We will have a pretty red spot on each cheek, and your eye-lashes picked out in black, and some blue for your lids. At least, that will give a little colour to your miserable features. I would hate the caliph to set eyes on you as you are now. He would wonder what sort of joke we were playing on him, sending him such a scarecrow."

A little later the empress said, "I do not know what Theodora was thinking of, putting you into the quarry. It has quite ruined your hands. You look more like a street-beggar than a noblewoman now. She could have had you whipped, couldn't she? That would have been more appropriate, wouldn't it? Well, am I to ask questions for ever, without getting an answer, girl? Don't you think whipping would have been more in keeping with your station, hey, child? It could have been done by one of our elevated officials. It need not have been done by the common executioner in the Hippodrome. Do you agree or don't you, Maria? Speak up now."

All at once Maria Anastasia fell to her knees and put her hands over her face. "Oh, Aunt Zoë," she sobbed, "I am so unhappy."

The empress waved her green fan at the sewing-women and sent them scuttling from the room. Then, half in mockery, half in genuine tenderness, she said, "Poor little scarecrow.

Not much of our ancient Greek pride runs in your blood, does it, my dear? No one would think you were of the kin of Alexander the Great, would they, little one?"

Then her voice hardened and she said, "Very well, get up now and stop creasing that new brocade with your pathetic rolling about on the floor. At least try to behave yourself with dignity and suffer in silence as we all must learn to do."

Maria stood up slowly and said, "You do not suffer, aunt; you only make others suffer."

The empress glowered at her for a moment, then she shrugged her heavy shoulders and said bitterly, "What do you know about suffering, you poor wretch? Just because we have sent your famous Northman away, you think you are suffering. Well, you must get used to the idea, Maria, because you will never see Harald Sigurdson again. He will not come back from Sicily alive, I think; but even if he does, you will be in another part of the world. No, do not begin that weeping all over again, I cannot bear it. Your face is ugly enough at its best, but with runnels of water down it, it is disgusting."

Suddenly Maria stopped crying and said quite fiercely, "Very well, Aunt Zoë, if you lack Christian charity towards me, I will appeal to the emperor. I will put my case before him and see if there is any justice left in Byzantium."

Then the empress got slowly off the couch and came towards the girl with a smile of malice on her powdered fleshy face. When she was an arm's length from Maria, she said, "You will appeal to Michael Catalactus, will you, child? And how far will such an appeal take you, do you think? Poor Michael is not long for this world, if you ask me, scarecrow. Have you noticed how thin he has got? How dark and staring his eyes are? How his hands shake when he holds the chalice in Hagia Sophia? No, of course you have not, because you are a fool whose head is filled with nonsense and whose eyes are blind to reality."

She turned away from the frightened girl, then suddenly swung round again and said viciously, "Why do you think he is so anxious to build his precious shrine in Jerusalem? I will tell you; it is because he knows that before long he must give an account to God of his stewardship of Christendom. He must have done one good thing, to balance all the evil things he has done and to avoid everlasting perdition. Can you hope for anything from such a poor tormented kingling, hey? Michael Catalactus is half out of his mind if a bird cries by his window in the darkness. Will you get any consideration from a sick fool whose head is stuffed with the terror of his own approaching doom? Go on, Maria Anastasia Argyra, you have my leave to approach the emperor for an audience. Ask of him what you please. But let me tell you this, the moment you have asked he will come to me, snuffling and shivering with agues, to find out my opinion on the matter. Well, what are you standing there for? Go and find the Most Serene Majesty."

Then Maria fell at her aunt's feet and clasped her robe. "Oh, empress," she said, "forgive me. But at least do not send me to the caliph, I beg you. Let me stay here, even in the quarry."

Zoë shook her green fan and said smiling, "You will not be advised, will you! You are willing to work on among slaves and gaol-birds just on the chance that the stupid great bear of a Norwegian comes back, aren't you! Well, let me tell you again, quite simply, that in this imperfect life we all must accept the realities about us, because the dreams exist only in our heads and are not real, however much we would like them to be so. The reality which you must accept is that you are soon to travel to Egypt and there help to seal the pact between our Holy Empire and the caliph. Nothing can change this, so you may as well get used to it without delay. As for your dream of Harald Sigurdson, if you are wise you will forget it from this moment, because whoever else you may meet in this world as your life goes on, you will never again see that Norseman."

Then the empress went back to her couch and rang a small silver bell that stood beside it. The six sewing-women ran into the chamber, their mouths full of pins, and went on with the dress-fitting as though nothing had interrupted them.

32 · Olaf's Counsel

Harald's fleet came to harbour in Crete in the midst of wintry gusts and squalls of rain. Three longships had been lost on the voyage from Sicily and those that limped into port at ancient Cydonia rolled and wallowed as though they were ready for the sea-bottom themselves.

But, of all miracles, Harald Hardrada stood at *Stallion*'s prow to bring that ship to its moorings and when the plank was down he was first ashore, although he leaned heavily on a crutch and had to stop many times before his feet were on dry land.

Then, without waiting for his henchmen, he spoke to the harbour-master who greeted him and said, "I have come for Maniakes. Direct me to him."

The official shook at the knees and began to stammer, seeing the gaunt figure of Hardrada towering above him, and seeing what manner of ghastly henchmen stood behind their captain. They were more like men from the grave than living sailors; and of them all Haldor was the most frightful to look on. The northern craftsmen who carved the dragons' heads for ship-prows had never in their wildest imaginings dreamed of such stark features.

Eystein said roughly, "You heard the captain, man, answer him. Where is Maniakes?"

Then the harbour-master cried out in foreboding, "He is not here, my lords. He was summoned to Byzantium almost a month ago, to answer to the emperor for something he had done, or not done. I do not know anything, my lords. I am not to blame."

Harald reached out and took the man by the beard and then drew him down to his knees. The Norseman's eyes gleamed red, as though he meant to put an end to the harbour-master there and then, on the wharfside of his own haven.

The man cried out, "My lord, my lord, all the world says that you are a just man, though a harsh one. I am only a port official. I have nothing to do with the vengeances of generals. Look, my lord, this Maniakes has been punished already. We have heard that all his titles and wealth have been taken from him and that the emperor has banished him to some place of barbarians beyond the Danube. He is a broken man now, my lord. I pray you, do not punish me for something which is not my affair."

Then Harald said, "A broken man, eh? Among the barbarians, eh? Well, it is a sort of vengeance, though it is not as sweet as the revenge a man takes with his own two hands."

He loosed the harbour-master's beard and let the poor wretch fall to the stones of the wharfside. Then he thought for a while and afterwards said, "Harbour-master, something you said has interested me. The world calls me a just man, though a harsh one, does it?"

The official put his hands together as though praying, but Harald smiled and said, "Nay, do not be afraid, I have this crutch for walking on, not for any other purpose. Speak your mind, speak your mind."

So the man said, "My lord, I spoke in terror. The world calls you a just man and a gentle one. That is what I meant to say."

Then Harald turned away from him and said to Wulf, "The fellow is a craven coward. If he had been man enough to repeat what he said at first, I would have given him a bag of gold as big as his fat head. But now we will use this place as our own. We will use it as our forefathers used Aachen and what we do not use we will burn. I have no patience with cowards."

But before Harald could hobble to his litter, a good-looking young man in the armour of the Byzantine Guard pushed through the frightened crowd and, taking off his helmet, bowed to the viking and said with all deference, "My lord, I am an equerry to the emperor. May I deliver his message to you without fear of your wrath?"

Harald looked the young man up and down for a time, then said, "From the brisk look of you, you will deliver it, wrath or not. How many battles have you been in?"

The young man said gravely, "I do not keep a tally, my lord. But I think it is twelve or so."

Then Harald said, "Were any of them against Bulgarians?"

The young man said with a smile, "Most of them, sir."

"Then," said Harald, "you have a right to speak among men. Give me Michael's message."

So the young soldier told Harald that he had been waiting on Crete for his arrival for over a month, and that the emperor commanded the Varangers to proceed to Jerusalem, and there to guard the Greek workmen who were soon to rebuild the Church of the Holy Sepulchre.

And when Harald had heard this command, he said to the young man, "Is this a plot to keep me away from Byzantium, do you think, soldier?"

The youth said, shrugging his shoulders, "Who am I to think of politics, my lord? I am a simple soldier."

Then Harald said shrewdly, "Tell me, simple soldier, how are things in Byzantium? Has this emperor a good strong Greek army about him nowadays?"

The soldier smiled up at him slyly and said, "Sir, I did not speak very plainly before, I am afraid. I am suffering from toothache brought on by standing at the harbourside, waiting for your ships to come over the horizon. So, I will repeat, I know nothing of politics. They are for great men and I am a simple soldier."

Then Harald said, "You are certainly no spy, I can tell that. Very well, simple soldier, how would you like to come aboard my ship and fight for me?"

The young man bowed his head and said, "If my oath of fealty were not already given to the emperor, nothing would please me better, my lord."

Then Harald said, "That was well answered, simple soldier. I would not try to entice any other man's watchdog. May good luck always go with you, my friend, and one day may it bring you a general's staff of command. But one word of advice—do not loiter about at harboursides in future. Toothache is the worst thing for a soldier to suffer, it takes his mind off his job."

The young man said, "I shall remember your advice, sir. And I thank you for it."

And when he had gone, Eystein said to Harald, "So, when we have rested and revictualled, we go to Jerusalem, hey?"

But Harald clenched his teeth grimly and answered, "No, brother. Jerusalem may rot for all I care now. When we have rested we shall take the sea-road north towards Byzantium and burn that evil place to the ground. If I cannot take my vengeance on Maniakes, then I will get it on those who first set that mad dog on me."

And when he had said this, Harald seemed to grow older and to sink into the deepest gloom that any man could recall.

From this time, throughout the winter, Harald fell into such strange moods that the men declared he had sold his soul to the devil in return for the healing of his wound. Certainly the fever left him and his flesh knit well, leaving him little to show for Hauteville's blows but furrowed white scars; but his temper became so uncertain, and his sudden changes from laughter to roaring so frequent, that all but his oldest friends avoided him when they could.

For some reason he lost no chance to say harsh things to Eystein and Wulf, especially when the Varangers were present and listening; though he was as gentle as a mother to Haldor and Helge, and would let them speak words to him which no other man would have dreamed of.

One evening Wulf said to Eystein, "He is not the man we sailed with. How long we can bear his strange ways I do not know. If it weren't for Haldor I would leave now and smell my way back to Iceland. But when we started out to see the world, I promised Haldor's mother that I would never leave his side while there was life in me."

Eystein answered, "It is part of Harald's sickness, brother. The flesh has healed but there is a great wound in his spirit yet. But come fair, come foul, we have taken the oath to serve him and that we must do, though he should sprout horns in the night. Let us say no more."

They had scarcely finished speaking when Helge came and said, "He wants to see you both. Do not blame me for his tantrums, brothers, but I know better than to tell the Bear he is a fool when he strokes me with sheathed claws."

So they saw how it was and went with Helge. Harald smiled at them this time and said, "I have been thinking; here we are, after months of hardship, revengeless and unpaid. This is not Greek justice, my friends. I mean to see that all the Varangers get their back-pay. First we will sack the treasury here and then we will put a tax on all the folk of Cydonia, men, women and children. They shall pay for drawing breath in this city. The oldest shall pay the least because they have the shortest time left to breathe. But the babies shall pay the most, for the opposite reason. And the girl-babies shall pay more than the men-babies, for it is well known that women outlive men for the most part."

Wulf said outright, "Harald, this is madness. Sack the treasury if you will, but this tax on breathing God's air is the sort of thing that will make you seem a lunatic in the eyes of the world."

He had said it before Eystein could stop him. Now the words were out, flying free, and Harald snorted so deeply that he seemed about to choke.

Then, with a deathly face and a whistling voice, Harald said, "Who is this man who thwarts me? Tell me his name, the name of this man?"

Eystein tried to calm him, but always Harald kept saying, "Tell me his name, the name of this man." Until at last Wulf jumped up and said, "You know my name well enough, Sigurdson. We have been side by side for years now, and if you do not know me then you are indeed the biggest fool in Christendom."

Helge came close to Harald to catch him if he tried to wrestle with Wulf; but suddenly the Bear of Norway shuddered as though they had thrown ice-cold water over his head and said more quietly, "Very well, brothers, the matter is settled then. Bring me all the coin that lies in the treasury, and keep all the gold and silver-ware for the men's back-pay. We will forget the breath-tax for the time being. I did not like the idea myself when Eystein suggested it to me."

So the treasury was sacked, and Harald commandeered one of the longships to take his great share northwards to Kiev and put it in the care of King Jaroslav, to whose daughter Harald was betrothed.

A month after this Harald sacked the treasury of Tarrha and took yet another ship to transport his own raven's pickings northwards. Then he burned down three villages between

Phaestus and Mount Ida because the peasants refused to pay a new hoof-tax on cattle and sheep that he had thought of.

Now Wulf said secretly to Eystein, "I almost wish that Hauteville had struck up more sharply that day in the wood. He is giving us a bad name in the world. Have you noticed, when we go out into the countryside now, we see no men, no women, no sheep and cattle—nothing. It is as though everything vanishes as we go forward. I do not like it, brother."

Eystein said, "I have always gained my bread and meat honestly before; perhaps hard, but honestly. So have my shipmates. We do not profess to be the best Christians in the world, but we have no stomach for this village-burning. The cries of the women and children sound in our dreams."

Then Wulf said, his eyes full and brimming, "Brother, you know me now almost as well as a man could. I am not a particularly bloody man, but it is being sharply driven home to me that unless Harald is curbed, then the world will spit when his name is mentioned. There is only one way to curb him, Eystein." And as he said this, he drew his dirk from the banding on his right leg. It was a stark weapon, the length of a man's forearm, broad at the haft and coming in to the sticking-point, with runnels all its distance to give it lightness in the blade. Its handle was yellow walrus ivory from off Greenland, riveted with iron nails. No man would say that it was the prettiest pig-sticker in the world, but there was none deadlier. The iron of its edges was black, and it had never been re-ground.

Eystein looked at it sideways, as fighting-men do at such wicked things, then said, "Put it away, brother. I don't like these things."

So Wulf put it away, but his mind was made up.

A week later an old woman brought in for questioning told Harald that she came from the ancient mountain of Dicte, where she claimed Zeus was born to his mother Rhea. Harald made her stand close to him and said, "This birth-place, what was it, a fine palace?"

The old crone laughed and answered, "No, viking, we have no palaces up there. It was a cavern. And I can tell you, in that cavern we have found such things!"

Harald took her by the shoulder and drew her squirming towards him. "What things, old woman?" he said.

She cried out, "Oh, master, do not hurt me!"

He said again, "What things, old woman? Answer quickly."

And she said, "Oh, oh! Precious things! Magic things! Axes and swords, sir!"

He let her go then and said, "Give her food and drink, but no money. These peasants do not understand money as we do. Then send her packing."

So Harald took the notion of finding the cavern of Zeus as a greedy fish takes the baited hook.

And when spring came, the Varangers went to Mount Dicte, and there found an immense cave of limestone, with a massive hall, and then a chasm that fell steeply for two hundred feet into the darkness. Eystein and Wulf led thirty men down there on ropes and found that there was a black pool at the foot of the drop. And then, hall after hall, decorated by great stone columns from floor to roof, and all created by nature. But the only thing they brought back up to the daylight was a little bronze brooch on which had been cast the shapes of a woman in a flounced skirt and a palm tree.

When the party came up, Harald asked, "Where are the axes and swords?"

But Eystein stuck him out and said, "This is all there was. If you do not believe us, go down yourself and see." He spoke out boldly, almost as though to an enemy.

So Harald took this brooch and said scornfully, "It will do well enough to hold up my third-best cape. It is too small to support a cloak."

Wulf said then, "I should look more closely at it if I were you, Sigurdson. You may find that it bears a message on it. It may foretell your doom." He too spoke out boldly, with little love sounding in his voice.

Harald smiled pleasantly then and squinted at the brooch. "No," he said, "it is only a woman dancing under a tree."

"Then," answered Wulf grimly, "you have nothing to fear."

Harald said, "The darkness has turned your mind, brother. What is there in a woman, or a tree, for that matter, to make any man afraid?"

Wulf said, "Aye, to be sure, what is there?"

So they made the journey back to Cydonia. And there Harald drank too much of the wine of that place and as he sat with Haldor by the brazier, suddenly saw that Olaf his half-brother who had died at Sticklestad was standing at the far side of the room, where the shadows were thickest.

Harald said, half-rising from his stool, "Why, brother, they did not tell me you were in Crete. I should have been down at the harbour to greet you."

But Saint Olaf put on a very hard face and said, "Do not get up, Harald. You will fall on your face if you do."

Harald began to laugh, but Olaf silenced him with a stiff glare and then said, "Now, you are hardly the brother I knew years ago, when the Dane-king came against us. Do not try to explain anything to me, I already know it all. So listen, for I shall not be with you long, since I have other more important things to attend to than thieves and traitors."

Harald began to frown at these words but he was fixed by the wine on his stool and had to listen. Then Olaf said, "Our mother will be proud of you, will she not? She will wish to know that you have betrayed the emperor to whom you bowed the knee. She will smile when she hears of the burned villages, no doubt. And she will laugh outright when she is told that you wish Jerusalem may rot so that you can send shiploads of stolen rubbish up to Kiev while your comrades in Christendom are dying in their war against the infidel."

Harald waited a while, then said to his brother, "Olaf, there are some things that not even you can understand. You have been away so long."

But Saint Olaf answered as starkly as ever: "I have seen all, and understand all. I am not named Haldor or Helge, who worship every sound you make. Remember who I am, and hearken to me, for it will be long enough before I come again, little brother."

Then Harald said humbly, "Say on, brother, I am listening."

And Olaf answered starkly, "That is just as well. Now forget all your revenges and coin-grasping, and go as soon as the winds will take you to the Holy Sepulchre they are building in Jerusalem. Do this without fail, or I will not claim kinship with you again."

Harald nodded obediently, then said, "But the brooch, with the woman and the palm tree on it. Tell me, what does it mean?"

Then as he faded back through the dim wall, Olaf said, smiling at last, "Go to Jerusalem and find out yourself, you lazy fellow."

Harald shook himself and said to Haldor, "Did you see anything?"

Haldor only stared at him vacantly, then mumbled, "I saw a mouse look out from under your stool, then run away into the corn-bin over there. Is that what you mean?"

Harald laughed now. "Aye," he said, "maybe that was what I meant, brother. Come, let us get our gear ready for Jerusalem. We have been too long already obeying our emperor. Now there is man's work to be done."

33 · Jerusalem

So summer came again into the life of Harald Sigurdson. The winter he had passed through had left its mark on him, truly enough, for now he was like a sword-blade that has passed through the fire to be hammered by the smith to a new hardness. He laughed less than before, was sharper with the Varangers and more ruthless in any task he set his hand to. But he had come out of the tunnel of his madness and soon his name as a fair-dealing captain had spread again so widely that young voyagers from the northern lands flocked to serve him, like peasant-women gathering about a trader's market-stall to gain a bargain.

Even the caliph sent an envoy to him in Jerusalem, wishing him God's help in the work that now lay before him. Harald listened while the envoy read his master's words aloud, then said, "I have no scribe and I cannot write; but take back this message to your lord: tell him that Harald Sigurdson is here for two purposes only—to protect the masons who will build a church to the glory of God, and to clear all roads of such robbers, of whatever land or faith, as hinder decent pilgrims who would pray in the Holy City or bathe in the Jordan. And tell the caliph that Harald Sigurdson wishes no gain for himself or his men, more than their soldiers' pay which comes from their emperor in Byzantium. And make it clear to him that these men are not lawless foragers, but Christian guards who will work side by side with his own lawgivers and police to restore the good name of Palestine."

And when Harald had finished the envoy smiled and said, "I will report your words faithfully, my lord. Or at least as faithfully as they will fit into our own language."

Harald said, "I ask no more, sir. It is not the words that matter but the good heart that lies beyond the words."

In the months that followed Harald set up garrisons in Tripoli, Damascus, Jaffa and Ascalon, as well as in Jerusalem itself. This was done with the consent of the Saracen governors of these cities and there were no quarrels. Such was the good feeling at this time between Christian and Muslim that many of the Varangers swore that they would willingly have followed the Prophet's law themselves, but for the fact that he forbade the drinking of wine. As it was, the two peoples became firm friends, exchanged gifts and even war gear. So that at last it was hard to tell whether a man was Christian or Muslim save by drawing back the chain-flap of his helmet and looking at the colour of his skin. And all the while the new Church of the Holy Sepulchre rose, stone by stone; and the Byzantine masons and their Syrian helpers sang at their work, unafraid.

But there were those at whom fear struck; these were the desert Bedouin whose ancient fierce custom was to lurk among the sand dunes waiting for pilgrim processions, and then to rush out, robbing and murdering the helpless Christians. Before long the Bedouin discovered painfully that their own fast camels or horses were now matched by other camels and horses just as fleet, ridden by men as merciless as themselves, and far better fighters with sword, spear and axe.

Harald made it a practice to hang all Bedouin caught stealing, in rows, without trial. And once hoisted, he left their bodies to dangle as a ghastly warning to any other desert scavenger who had it in mind to gain easy pickings from innocent pilgrims.

Soon the Bedouin faded away from all the main routes, to seek their livelihood elsewhere. Then pilgrims came in droves from Hungary and Poland, France, England, Germany and Italy. And the caliph welcomed this as much as any man, for his frontier officials levied a poll-tax on all Christians who came into the Holy Land to visit shrines or to bathe in the Jordan.

After a while, Wulf said to Harald one day, "Brother, you have now tamed this land so sternly that it seems our work is done here. We could set up scarecrows along the routes, dressed in Varanger gear, and leave them to drive away the robbers while we went on a jaunt to Mosul to see if our old friend the emir is still alive and well."

Harald said, "I think of him often. He is one of the good men I have met in my life, and there have not been too many such. We cannot all withdraw from our duties, but at least a score of us who knew the old man might take a holiday from this task and ride northwards, leaving the command of the Varangers here in the hands of Helge, who will one day be a great man in Byzantium when we have gone home."

And this is what they set out to do, laying aside their helmets and hauberks, and wearing the white flowing robes of Saracens, with their war gear drawn behind them in ox-wagons so that they might ride in comfort.

But when they were twenty miles north of Jerusalem, on a lonely stretch of desert road, they saw galloping towards them a messenger wearing the imperial Greek insignia. If they had not drawn across the road to halt him, he would have fallen anyway, for his horse was spent with hard riding.

And after they had revived the messenger so that he could talk some sort of sense, Haldor said to him in his gruff way, "Well, friend, what is your news? It must be that Rome is burning from the way you ride."

The man shook his head and answered, "Not Rome, Northman, but perhaps Byzantium by this time."

Harald was thinking of his men's pay and said, "Make yourself plain, man. We cannot guess Greek riddles, only Norse ones."

Then the messenger said, "I think that the world is coming to an end at last, sir. And the first warning God gives us is that He has made our rulers mad. With no one to guide us, how can we Byzantines guide the rest of the world?"

Wulf came up and took the man by the shoulder and shook him. "Now take your time," he said, "and tell us this story from the beginning. You should know that stories do not begin at the end, for you Greeks have told more stories in your time than any other folk, even Orkneymen."

Then the rider took a deep breath and said, "Here, then, is the list of disasters. Michael Catalactus has died, of sickness or poison or smothering in his bed—we do not know, and it was not safe to enquire. Then the widow Zoë, after weeping her public tears, raised her dead husband's nephew, the one they call Michael Calaphates, to the status of emperor and enthroned him herself. But little did she know the quality of the man, for his first act was to throw her into prison, in a convent on the island of Prinkipo."

Harald drew in his breath, then said with a hard smile, "This Michael Calaphates is a young man of good sense. He can see further than the last two emperors of Byzantium."

At this the messenger began to laugh bitterly. "There you are wrong, captain," he said. "He cannot see at all now. The citizens of Byzantium rose in a great rebellion and released Zoë from her cell. Her great pride was so hurt by this Calaphates that she had him blinded and put into a monastery to drag out his days. Now she and her mad sister Theodora reign as joint-empresses and do as they please."

Harald said, "I do not mind, as long as they please to pay my army out here. As for the rest, these empresses may please themselves. It is no concern of ours."

The messenger laughed again and said, "What I now have to deliver concerns you very closely, sir. These empresses command you to return to Byzantium straightway, to answer for all your actions."

Harald sat back on a rock and slapped his thigh with merriment. "They command me!" he said. "Those two stupid women command me! I might see it in my heart to obey an emperor to whom I had sworn allegiance—but to two women, who are more concerned with perfumes and prayers than with ruling an empire properly! No, my friend, that is not the sort of command Harald Sigurdson listens to."

The messenger said, "So, you will not return to Byzantium, captain?"

Harald answered, "Oh, yes, I will return, certainly. But not as they think to have me, grovelling before them alone. I shall withdraw all the Varangers from Palestine to go and greet these empresses; and we shall see which side of their faces they laugh on when we put into haven in the Golden Horn."

The rider said, "Then I will take that message back to them."

But Harald nodded to Wulf and Eystein, who took the man by the arms and tied his wrists to his saddle-horn. Then he said, "No, my friend, we shall take the message back ourselves. As for you, your duties are over for the time being. We shall put you in the charge of certain Saracen friends we have in Jerusalem, and they will care for you well until we are sailing through the Sea of Marmara."

The messenger nodded and smiled. "Thank you, sir," he said. "I had no great wish to take back such a reply as you have spoken."

34 · The Bronze Brooch

Riding into Jerusalem the Varangers were silent, each ot them turning over in his mind the great step they were about to take in making war against the holy city of Constantinople. But they were with Harald to a man. And so were the garrison commanders assembled in Jerusalem at that season. As the captain of Ascalon said, "If we do not stand firmly together now against these mad women, they will use us like slaves for the rest of time. A man must stand up for himself; but a Norseman must stand up like two men."

They sent out swift riders straightway, ordering all Varanger garrisons to withdraw and to meet a week later, fully prepared to sail out from Jaffa, where the northern fleet lay at anchor.

And when all this was arranged, Harald said to his battle-brothers, "I shall now go to the Saracen emir here in Jerusalem and put our case plainly before him, telling him that when we have settled affairs in Byzantium to our satisfaction, we shall return until such time as the Church is built."

Wulf, Haldor, Helge and Eystein all agreed that this was the way an honest man should act, and they walked out with Harald towards the square where the emir had his quarters, wearing their swords, helmets and cloaks now, but not their hauberks, for the evening was oppressive after the day's sultry heat.

But when they got to the place where the masons were still working on the scaffolding, using what light was left to them, they halted. A long black-robed procession of women stood by the main door of the Church, wailing and throwing dust over their heads as though in penance. In the middle of the crowd stood a black-draped litter with silver lions' feet. Its four posts were also of silver, but shaped like palm-trunks, with fronds of jasper stretching out above the curtains.

Haldor said gruffly, "I cannot bear the sound women make, wailing. It would set my teeth on edge if I had any teeth left worth mentioning."

Wulf said, "They have lost someone, or are about to do so."

Helge said, "They are Armenians or Druzes, by that strange

black they wear. They are certainly not any folk I have ever seen before. They are strange creatures, these foreign women. But very interesting."

Eystein said, "You must be as blind as poor Michael Calaphates, for even I recognize three of these women. They are the ladies Euphemia, Anna and Sophia from the Inner Court at Byzantium."

Harald said, "Then by the Grace of God we may not have to travel as far as the city to ask the empress what game she is playing. She may even now be sitting within our grasp! She may be among them, wailing!"

He started forward, ignoring the two hooded horsemen who kept a watch on this procession, their long lances in their hands, and hurried to the rich litter. Pushing aside the veiled women who were in his way, he bent forward and switched back the drapes, his mouth already open to speak words of anger.

Then he stopped and for an instant almost let fall the curtains. Gazing back at him, dark-eyed and pale-faced with sorrow, was Maria Anastasia Argyra, dressed like one dedicated to a life of endless mourning. The red spots painted on her cheeks only served to stress their whiteness and to make the reality of her sadness grotesque.

Yet as soon as she saw Harald, her eyes lit up and her pale lips smiled. Now she almost leapt from that dark litter and flung her arms about him. "Why, viking," she cried, "you are here! They told me you had died in Sicily. But you are here!"

The women stopped wailing and turned to gaze speechlessly as their princess hugged the great Norseman. The two hooded riders began to spur forward, their lances lowering, but Eystein went to the first of them and touched him politely on the thigh. "If you know when your luck is with you, friend," he said calmly, "you will take a turn round the square before you point those skewers at anyone in Jerusalem. The big man with the golden beard is master here. Someone should have told you. You are not in Bulgaria now, friends."

The lancers backed their horses off and drew against the wall farthest away from the procession, frowning under their hoods.

Harald said, "So it is the little girl who rode on my shoulders once. And where are you going?"

Maria Anastasia said simply, "I am going with you, captain."

The viking answered, "But we are bound for Byzantium, lady. And we shall travel rough over the sea. That would not suit you. Besides, we have no room in the longships for all these women of yours, these wailers."

Maria Anastasia said, "I would travel to the moon with you in a tub. As for these women, most of them never wish to set eyes on Byzantium again. They will be happy enough to be left here with the two Bulgars to guard them. Husbands are arranged for them in Cairo."

But Haldor said sternly, "I was never in favour of taking women aboard, Harald. They can bring misfortune to a vessel. It is not our custom."

But Maria turned on him sharply and said, "I do not know who you are, sir, but it is news to me that a mere rover can out-talk his captain."

Wulf said laughing, "Oh yes, you do know who it is, princess. It is Haldor, the viking who came with Harald and myself that first day to the palace. He looks a bit different now, but that is because he has been worrying about certain things. Worry changes a man's expression."

Then Maria put her hand on Haldor's arm and said, "Oh, Haldor. I am so sorry. But indeed you look handsomer than ever. Now you look as I have always imagined the great kings of Valhalla must have looked. The grand ones, the black-faced troll kings. There is not a noblewoman in Byzantium, or Rome, who would not swoon at the sight of you, Haldor."

Haldor turned away abruptly and muttered, "Let her come, Harald. I have misjudged the girl. She has more sense than women usually have."

So Harald smiled down at Maria and said, "You have heard his judgement. And I did swear once that I would take you with me to where you wished to go. So if you are not afraid of hunger and sea-drenchings, then you may come."

And when he had said this, Maria Anastasia Argyra picked up her heavy flounced skirt and began to dance with joy under the silver palm tree with their jasper fronds.

Then all at once Harald felt inside his pouch and drew out the little bronze brooch he had brought up from the cave of Zeus and stared at it closely. To himself he said, "So, Olaf, you knew this would happen all along—you sly old saint! You sly old Christian, you!"

Maria halted breathlessly and said, "What have you got in your hand, viking? Is it a lucky charm?"

Harald shrugged his broad shoulders and said, "Aye, you could say that of it, in a way. Although at one time I did not think so."

Then he put it into her hand and said smiling, "It is for you, princess. It is a present from Crete. Perhaps, many lifetimes ago, it belonged to one of your ancestors, who knows? In any event it is yours now, and may it always bring you good fortune. Failing that, it will do to pin up your skirts when you next go dancing under palm trees!"

Maria Anastasia began to weep as she held his arm; but this time her tears were those of joy. It had been a long while since anyone had given her a present without asking something in return for it.

35 · "We Shall Be Dead!"

Twelve days out, standing off Chios against a contrary wind, Haldor said with a grey look in the eye, "It comes to me more and more as we journey, that this is the last time I shall sail up through the Islands."

Wulf said, "I had the same feeling as we rounded Samos. I put it down to the salted pork we have been eating, which is none of the freshest now, and I forgot all about it. Now you make me remember that feeling again and I agree with you. It will be the last time. I am sure of that now."

Harald was lounging beside them at the gunwale and said, "I once heard two old butterwomen on Stronsay ranting about which one would die first. They each had had a dream the night before and they came to blows for the privilege of being the first to have the church bell rung for them. You two sound like those women. I have heard ravens on a battlefield, the morning after, which sounded merrier—aye, far merrier."

Haldor half-turned and looked at him with wrinkled eyelids like an old eagle and said, "You are reckoned to be a strangely brisk young fellow, aren't you, Sigurdson?"

Harald plucked a bit of fur from his cape and blew it up into the air to watch the wind carry it backwards from the ship. He looked down at Haldor, his light eyes smiling, and said, "I have heard some such. Though I have never said so. It is what people say. The man himself does not say it."

Haldor said, "Very well, if you are as brisk as men say, you will not take this fleet into the Golden Horn, young briskling. You will head on up the Bosphorus to the Holy Mouth and out into the Black Sea and home."

Harald said with innocence, "And why should I do that, having vowed to shake sense into these empresses and to burn their old rabbit-warren about their ears?"

Haldor answered, "Because, although I am no longer a brisk young fellow, I still have a nose for the scent of death."

Then Wulf joined him and added, "It has been in my nostrils for days, brother. There is no mistaking it once you have smelled it."

Maria was standing a few yards away with her handmaiden, Euphemia, teasing blue wool from a spindle. She came forward and said, "I have heard what you men have been saying. I must now tell you that I too have had some sort of dread as we have got nearer and nearer to Byzantium. It is like entering the spider's web. Can we not do as they say, Harald, and sail on to safety in the Black Sea? I would love to see the north. I have heard of it all my life, but have only seen the hot sun and our grapes and melons. I would love to stand in an icy wind on a green mountain, with the great grey sky roaring over my head. Oh, Harald, can we not go to the north? I would adore the north."

Harald Sigurdson turned round very slowly as though he did not know who was speaking; and when he had turned he made a great pretence of not being able to see the speaker, because she was so small. And when he had gone through all this game, at which only he was the smiler, he said, "I wonder if I did wrong after all to bring you aboard? They say women are unlucky."

Maria said quite sharply, "Often in this life it takes a woman to tell men what sense is. Men are like little boys, only bigger, who still need to be told when to put on their warm clothes or to wash their hands."

Harald said, "I have got on my warmest fur cape and my hands are clean. What is the argument, woman? What have you to tell me?"

Maria stamped her foot with impatience and said, "It is the very simple matter of death, great captain. If you go to Byzantium you could be dead, like that!" As she spoke, she snapped her thumb and middle finger together with a click.

Harald watched this and smiled. "Do that again, my princess," he said, "it made a pretty sound. Yes, do it again. I like it."

But Maria snorted and turned away from him in irritation. Then she and Euphemia went to the after-cabin of *Stallion,* which had been turned into a bower for them on this voyage.

So Harald turned to Haldor and Wulf with a stark flat look about his eyes and said like iron, "If you two old butter-women start such a conversation again you had better be prepared to swim the rest of the way because, as sure as Thor made hammers, I'll pitch you both neck and crop into the sea. That is my last word."

Then he turned and left them to go and pour ale for the rowers, who were at the end of their tether against such a body-buffeting wind from the north.

And when he had gone out of earshot Wulf said, "The girl was right, Haldor. She may only be a princess with blue wool in her hand but she was right. We should not go on, for it will be our deaths. It is the spider's web."

Haldor was picking a splinter out of his thumb and did not look up. He said absently, "Aye, for a Greek this Maria is not without sense. I met a Saracen lass once, an emir's daughter from Jebel Tarik, who spoke much the same way and didn't look too unlike this Maria. They are very similar, these outlanders down here. Dress them up this way or that way and I cannot tell one from the other until they open their pretty pink mouths."

Wulf struck the gunwale till the shields rattled and said, "I am not talking about girls, you Iceland-fool. I am talking about life and death."

Haldor said, "Oh, are you, brother? And what did you decide? I am always willing to listen to wise men giving their judgement."

Wulf gazed at him speechlessly for a while, then drew in a very long breath and said through locked teeth, "If we go to Byzantium, brother, we shall be dead—like this!"

He clicked his thumb against his middle finger and the sound he made was like that which Maria had made but very much louder and sharper. Very much louder and sharper, and colder.

36 · The Second Song

On the way northwards to the Hellespont Harald made ten songs. They were not the best he had ever made, but this is the best of them.

I yearn for the grey stones of Norway
Shaded by green trees;
And the gnarled pines sighing
In a bitter breeze.

I long to sit by spruce fires
When the ale-cup passes round,
And to hear a tongue spoken
That I can understand.

If I live to be a hundred
And my sense stays sharp,
I shall never forget Gyric,
I shall never cease to weep.

The Second Song

They call me Sigurdson,
And Olaf was my brother;
He fell at Stiklestad.
Now there is no other.

To tell me what to do,
To tell me what to be.
I am the Bear of Norway,
Chained though free.

Maria heard this song and said, "You will never live to be a hundred if you put in at Byzantium. You will be chained, certainly, but will not get free."

Young Helge who was whittling a stick by the mast-stepping said smiling, "This is not the court poetry you are used to, lady. This is only rough northern stuff that helps men to find the beat of the oars as they row. You are not meant to find pretty things and wisdom in our songs. They are for men."

Maria answered, "The more's the pity. Harald should make a song that gives the men such a desire to be back home that they could not bear to put into port anywhere until they were safe in the Dnieper on the way to Kiev."

Haldor was watching Helge carving the stick and said, "Safe? Safe? Who would sleep well in his bed or eat well at the board, thinking that he set safety before his proper duty as a man?"

Maria said, "Only a few days ago you were advising Harald to sail past the Holy City and into the Black Sea. Now you have changed your tune."

Haldor nodded glumly. "Oh aye," he said, "but that is the way of things. Did you ever know the wind to blow three days together from the same quarter?"

Maria clenched her hands in annoyance. "Oh, you Northmen," she said. "When will you learn sense?"

Wulf said, "Never, princess. That is why we are Northmen."

So she gave up trying to talk to them and went with Euphemia into the cabin-bower to pray for them. They were such fools, such children.

The ships rounded the Horn and put in to harbour a month after leaving Palestine. Byzantium looked very bright and white and full of splendid high towers, after so long on the water. But Maria said, "My Aunt Zoë can look very grand but beneath her splendour she is as cruel as the Egyptian crocodile."

Harald laughed and said, "Her days of cruelty are numbered, little one. When we march up to the palace and kick the door in she will grovel like any lesser creature. She will cry and beg for mercy and then you will see what stuff even great empresses are made of. They are all the same once they see the sword grinning out of its scabbard."

Wulf had been gazing shorewards all this time. He said, "It seems that half of Byzantium is out to see us come into anchorage. I have never seen so many folk before. We must be heroes."

Haldor said, "These folk have little better to do. They would turn out and crowd the walls just to watch two dolphins sporting. When I am king in Constantinople, I shall pass a law to make every man and woman do a fair day's work. My own people up in Iceland have to work for their bread so why should these Byzantines laze their days away? Helge, on that stick of yours, carve a rune to remind me that when I am king. . . ."

Maria said very solemnly, "You will never be king of anywhere, Haldor. If you step ashore here you stand a better chance of being a corpse."

Harald patted her on the arm and, smiling grimly, said, "Now, now, lady. That is no way to put ambition into a brisk young fellow like our Haldor. You do not know Icelanders yet, it seems. If they say they will be caliphs in Cadiz—then that is what they will be or know the reason why."

Maria put on her expression of *dignitas* to go ashore. She whispered, "He will never know the reason why, and nor will you, Sigurdson."

Then the men lowered the plank and all out of *Stallion* strode to the wharfside as proudly as they could, to give the crowds a good show.

And as soon as all the Varangers were ashore, a tall young officer with pale yellow hair came forward and held up his right hand in greeting to them. He said loudly for all to hear, "I am Guttorm Fis, Captain of the Varangian Guard in Miklagard. I come from Sweden."

Haldor said, "Where is Thorgrim Skalaglam? We left him as captain when we went away."

The Swede smiled and said coldly, "Captains change like everything else in this world. The man you speak of went for a ride on four horses in the Hippodrome and never came back. Now, tell me, which of you is Sigurdson?"

Wulf glanced back to where Harald towered two heads above all others and then said to the Swede, "He is that little man over there with the golden beard. You will have to shout up, he is a bit deaf and cannot hear a mouse whispering. You must at least cry out like a rat, Swede!"

Guttorm Fis went very red about the neck and pushed past Wulf roughly on his way to Harald. Then he said, "Sigurdson, I am commanded to meet you and to conduct you to the imperial palace, where you are awaited."

Harald looked round at the three hundred guards who stood behind the new captain, then said, "I know the way. I have been here before. I do not need three hundred guides. I shall come in my own time. I have the sudden wish to wander along the wharfside and to buy a few melons for my men. It is a warm day and they are thirsty."

But Guttorm Fis said stubbornly, "The thirst and the melons will wait. I am commanded to conduct you to the palace straightway." He thrust out his jaw.

Helge lounged up to Harald and said, smiling, "Shall I knock this flax-distaff on the head, captain? He seems to have forgotten his manners."

Harald said, "Why put yourself to that trouble, brother? No, we will go with the little fellow after all, just to please him. Otherwise I can see that he will shed a few tears; and that would not be the best thing to do in front of all these gaping Greeks."

Yet, in his heart, Harald knew that he had to go with Guttorm Fis, for now so many other guards had filed on to the wharf that the sea-rovers were outnumbered by three to one, and moreover were weary from their long voyage and hardly likely to give the best account of themselves they would wish, if put to the axe-stand with the sea at their backs.

So, with Harald between two Swedes, and his northern brothers similarly guarded, they moved off. And now a new sight met their eyes as they passed the Acropolis and the Great Cistern; every square, avenue and even alley way was tight-packed with a black mass of Bulgar troops, fully-armed and stark-faced. No one had seen so many soldiers before.

Helge said, "What a fine homecoming! The empress seems to have assembled at least half of her hundred-thousand men to greet us."

Harald answered shortly, "She will still have to answer for Thorgrim Skalaglam. When I leave a captain-in-charge, I expect to see him again when I return, however long I may be away."

But Guttorm Fis only laughed, shortly and quietly, then said, "Hurry along, Sigurdson. They do not like to be kept waiting."

Harald said into his beard, "They have not much longer to

wait. When they see me, they will wish they had waited longer."

Then someone in the crowd behind the massed Bulgars screamed out, "Here they come, the sea-wolves! To the Hippodrome with them, the traitors!"

And another voice answered, "Yes, yes, hot irons are waiting."

Harald said to the Swede, "These fools seem to have made some mistake. They do not know who we are."

Guttorm Fis replied, "No, they have made no mistake. And they know who you are, well enough. They have been waiting for you these three months."

Then they were into the great courtyard of the palace and the tall bronze gates clanged shut behind them like the gates of doom.

Maria was crying openly now and had lost all her dignity of bearing. Her black skirts trailed in the dust like those of a peasant woman. She had had more pride when she hammered at the stones in the quarry of Saint Angelus.

37 · Trial and Judgement

They were no sooner inside the broad corridors of the palace than ten companies of Bulgars ran forward, armed with daggers, and hemmed them in so tightly that no man could draw his sword.

Guttorm Fis said to Harald pleasantly, "Now you must give up your weapons. You will not need them any more. They are just a burden."

Harald glared at him and said, "Why is this? In all our other homecomings we have carried our swords."

Guttorm Fis said, "Aye, but this is a different homecoming. In the Hall of Judgement no prisoner is permitted to carry a weapon of any sort."

Then Harald saw how it was, and called out to the rovers not to endanger their lives against such great odds by disobeying the order to hand over their edged tools.

To the Swede he said, "What is to become of us then, straw-hair?"

Guttorm Fis shrugged his shoulders and said without caring, "I have not been told that, Sigurdson. I simply had orders to trap the Bear, which I think you will admit I have done quite comfortably. Now my men and I are off duty and if you wish to know more you must ask the Bulgar captain. Though I do not think he will wish to tell you much. They are a sullen folk."

Harald drew in a deep breath, then said, "When I next come into Sweden, a few fires will redden the sky, make no mistake, straw-hair."

Guttorm Fis laughed openly at the hero now and said, "Our houses will be safe, Sigurdson. You will have no hands to strike flint on steel and no eyes to see whether your fires burn. Good day to you, old hero."

Then he turned smartly and drew his Varangers off into the open courtyard and away. The Bulgars who took over pushed and kicked the rovers along the corridors towards the Hall of Judgement. Some of the Northmen struck back and were knocked on the head with iron-shod staffs. So in the end they went as quietly as they could, but vowed to make the Bulgars pay for these blows as soon as they were out in the city again and free to move.

The Hall of Judgement was crowded with palace officials and noble spectators. The rovers were herded into the well of the court with Harald, Haldor, Wulf and Maria out in the front. Above them in a semi-circle sat the audience. And on a high dais before the spectators were set two splendid throne chairs.

Wulf said, "What do they think we are about to do—give a performance of some great play?"

A Bulgar who stood near them and could understand the Norse tongue said smiling, "You will perform, have no fear, although you do not know the words of the play as yet. It is an amusing drama, I can tell you. You learn the words as you go on. They are mostly screams."

Haldor said shortly to him, "No one spoke to you, Bulgar dog. Go back to your kennel and gnaw your bone."

The smiling Bulgar answered, "There will be bones, make no mistake. But they will be your bones. And I shall not gnaw them—the vultures will!"

Then there was a high blowing of trumpets and two heavily robed figures came slowly on to the dais and sat on the thrones. One was the Empress Zoë, and the other was an elderly man who had once been square-shouldered and tall but was now stooping and bent. His thin white hair hung down sadly under the high imperial crown. His long nose was red and he seemed to be perpetually sniffing. Two boys followed him to support the weight of his heavy cloth-of-gold robe.

Haldor said, "I expected to meet two empresses; not one empress and an old goat dressed in tinsel."

The Bulgar said, "What we expect and what we get in this life are two different things, sea-wolf. This is the new emperor, Constantine Monomachus. And if you are wise you will treat him with respect for though he is old his eyes and ears are sharper than a leopard's. He has a leopard's fangs and claws, too, as you will soon find out for yourselves."

Then a herald began to read at a great pace in legal Greek from a long roll of paper. The vikings could make nothing of this and fidgeted about until the Bulgar guards struck at them with the butts of lances and made them stand still and silent.

At last Harald could stand no more of this and called out,

"Sithee, Zoë, we are tired after a long journey. Let him tell us all this in plain language; then we will be off to eat our dinner."

The empress shuddered with annoyance but did not answer. Instead the new emperor Constantine Monomachus rose from his chair and, leaning on a gold staff, said in a strangely strong voice, "From your ridiculous height I know that it was Sigurdson who spoke so insultingly to his empress. Very well, if you want it in plain language you shall have it, in very plain language. In fact the language will be so plain that I doubt if you will be pleased with yourself for having called out so rudely when you have heard it."

Harald said back, "We came here to listen to sense, not to a red-beaked parrot chattering in a palm tree to amuse himself."

Then the silence in the high room was so great that it lay on all men's shoulders like a heavy load of lead.

And the new emperor said calmly, "Sigurdson, one-time Captain of the Varangian Guard in Byzantium, you have many charges to answer. You have made private and mutinous war for reasons of personal vengeance on one of our greatest generals, Georgios Maniakes. You have absented your army and much of our fleet in so doing, which amounts to mutiny also. You have fought with the Normans who have an alliance with us, and sided with the Saracens who are our old enemies. Furthermore, you have taken Crete on your own behalf, have burned its villages, have put its officials in a state of duress, have stolen imperial moneys and sent them to your own country. Finally, you have ruled in the Holy Land as though you were an emperor yourself, controlling the building of a church whose teachings you are not fit to follow. And, as if all this were not enough, you have abducted the princess Maria Anastasia Argyra, have deprived the Caliph of Egypt of her presence, and so have endangered the pact which we had vowed to observe with him. What have you to say to all this, in the hearing of this court?"

Harald scratched his head, smiled, and then said, "Whatever I said you would turn to your own ends, old goat. So why should I say anything?"

Beside him, Maria Anastasia was sobbing loudly now, so Wulf put his arm about her to comfort her. Immediately a Bulgar guard struck at him with a lance-shaft and knocked his hand down. Wulf whispered, "Thank you, my little monkey. Later today I will do the same for you and we shall see if you look so pleased with yourself then."

Constantine Monomachus saw this but made no comment. He waited a while, then said, "Our case is clear to all now. If we did not act firmly, we should be the foraging-place of all rough-chinned barbarians who wished to sail into Byzantium and use it like a midden. Has the court made up its mind about the verdict?"

He half-turned to a long bench at which sat twenty white-bearded old men in dark robes. One of them stood up and said, "It has, Most Serene Majesty. First, since among civilized people women must always come first, the lady Maria Anastasia Argyra is sentenced to a hundred strokes of the lash, to be awarded in public at the Hippodrome tomorrow. After which she is to be sent in chains to Egypt so that our pact may be upheld. As for the vikings, in all justice we cannot punish common men because their commanders go mad; so we have decided to confine them to barracks for a month and then put them on duty once more under the new captain. But as for their commanders, we must make an example or our reputation for correct dealing will be called into question throughout Christendom. Harald Sigurdson, Wulf Ospakson and Haldor Snorreson, being men of the greatest responsibility in our Varangian Guard, will suffer for all the others. The form of their suffering will be this—that they shall be taken to a strong gaol where they shall wait overnight without food or drink. And, having thus been given time to make their peace with God in prayer, they shall at dawn be taken to the Hippodrome and there punished in view of the people, as is right and proper. Harald Sigurdson, being the captain and therefore the most guilty by his infamous commands, shall lose eyes, tongue, and hands; the other two shall lose only their eyes and hands. All of them will then be taken back to prison where they will spend the remainder of their lives, short though that may be. And that is our decree, Most Serene Majesty."

And when this had been said and the old man had sat again, the emperor turned to Zoë and said, "Have you anything to say in mitigation of this judgement?"

Zoë looked above the heads of the vikings and then spoke in a loud clear voice. "Nothing," she said. "It is a just decree. Let them suffer."

38 · The Tower Prison

The Bulgars flung the three Varangers into a prison in a deserted part of the city, so that their mates should not know where to look for them. This prison was an old stone tower, open to the sky, with a door that led into the street, its many locks and bolts so rusted that no one would ever open it again. Inside the tower there was a spiral stairway that wound twelve feet up the wall and no further. The floor was dry and dusty, and littered with bones and feathers and the bodies of rats that the ants had picked clean. It was not the most pleasant place to be in.

For a time the three northern brothers did not speak to one another. Wulf and Haldor were very occupied with their hands, looking at them, and clenching and unclenching their fists, as though they were aware of them for the first time in their lives. Harald tried to walk up the winding stairway with his eyes tightly closed and his arms folded behind his back. Half-way up he lost his balance and fell down to the ground.

The others gazed at him for a while, then they all began to laugh. It was a stark laughter but it was some sort of sound to make, to use one's tongue.

Then Harald said, "I wonder if a prayer to my brother the Saint would do any good? When they were dragging us here I thought I saw him at a street corner, watching it all. It is strange how a man thinks such things when he is in trouble. I knew an Irish rover once who was wrecked and swam to a little rock skerry out in the open sea, where he stayed for three days and nights. He told me that at dawn each day he distinctly saw a longship heading towards that skerry with the shields all bright in the sun and the wind in the sail. But as soon as he shouted to it, the ship went into the sea-mist and disappeared."

Wulf said, "How did he get off the skerry, then?"

Haldor said, "I was just going to ask that."

Harald answered, "In the simplest way. He said a prayer and a great timber-log came floating by and he scrambled on to it and was in Galloway by the next day. But after all that, the fool went out the following week with some men from the Hebrides in a tarry curragh and got himself drowned among the little islands, in water he could almost have stood up in. That is fate."

Haldor said, "These tales do not make me merry. It would be more profitable if you went under the stairway and knelt down and said a prayer to your brother. I did not know him, so he would scarcely pay much attention to me. Besides, I am not good at speaking prayers unless there is a priest to lead the praying. I can never think of the right words."

Harald said, "Well, I will go, as you say; but you must not

expect too much to come from it. Where my brother Olaf is there will be many things to occupy his mind and I doubt whether he will look down very kindly on me, after what he said on Crete. I can tell you, he did not seem at all pleased with the way I had managed my life since he died at Stiklestad."

Wulf said, "He is a Saint, is he not? Very well, Saints are forgiving men. So go and pray. It may do no good—but it can do no harm. And there is nothing else we can do, unless we suddenly grow feathers on our arms and fly up out of this place."

So Harald went and prayed. The others turned their backs while he did this so as not to make him feel ashamed, kneeling in their sight.

And when he came back to them he said, "I do not know whether I did right or not, but I promised that if he would help us I would build a chapel to his memory on this street corner one day, when I was able."

Haldor said, "It never does any harm to make such a promise. At least it will show Olaf that you are trying to be a good Christian man."

Harald said, "Yes, I was at some pains to stress that to him in my prayer. I went further and told him that when I reached the north again I would really see that Trondheim got a new church to be proud of. The way we are now, Trondheim seems like another world, like a world in a dream; but it was worth saying and what is more I mean to do it if I am spared."

Wulf said, "It is amazing how we pray when we are in trouble. It is amazing how even a brave man will pray for mercy."

Harald said, "I have often wondered what this word 'brave' means. I have heard men call me brave, but I have never noticed what it was. The way I saw it, I was just a man, bigger than most men it is true, but just a man who had the good luck to knock the other men down."

Haldor nodded and said, "I have never thought much about it either. Although I have always been glad when I saw the other man lying at my feet."

Wulf said, "Before a battle, the palms of my hands always used to sweat."

Harald said, "You will not have that trouble any more after tomorrow. There is that to be said about it."

Wulf said, "No, but seriously, did your hands sweat before a battle, brother?"

Harald said, "Aye, and my legs used to shake so much I had to get moving into the fray in case I fell down before things started. I was a real coward."

Haldor said, "Mine did too. It was as though they were saying, 'Hurry, hurry, and let us begin.' I once knew a bare-sark from Thorsmork whose legs shook so much that his mates had to carry him to the battle and set him down in the middle of it or he would never have got there. He shuddered with terror."

Wulf said, "Do you remember old Hrut Herjolfsson who fell in love with the witch, Queen Gunnhild? He could never speak before a battle. He used to put his head down and cry like a girl. But once he had taken the first blow, even if it was no more than a slap on the cheek, he roared and jumped in like a lion, and was always the last to stop. But afterwards he cried all night."

Harald said, "Nay, I don't know what brave means. I think it is just a word that the scalds have made up. Let us talk about something else."

So they talked for a long time, trying not to mention hands and eyes. Though they always seemed to come round to them in the end.

Then a brown bird swooped into the open tower, struck it-self against the stone wall and fell to the ground. Haldor went and picked it up and felt its wings to find out if they were broken. They were pleased that the little bird was only stunned and passed it from one to the other gently to find out how it was made. Harald said, "This little bird does not own a sword or a helmet or a horse or a ship; yet he has something we all envy. He has wings. And they will get him out of here without any prayers to Saints."

He loosed the little brown bird, which flew straight up and away into the sky, without saying a word of thanks to them.

Wulf said, "I wonder if Olaf sent that bird to tell us we shall fly out over the top as he did?"

Haldor answered, "I find no feathers growing on my arms yet, brother. Although I have been feeling for them this last hour."

Harald said, "No, it was just a bird. Though I am glad we were here to pick it up when it lay stunned on the ground. Otherwise a rat might have come up out of one of those holes and have made a meal of it."

Wulf said, "I have no objection to a fox eating a partridge, if he can catch one. Or an eagle eating a hare, if he is brisk enough to swoop on one. But I cannot bear to see these little creatures tearing at one another. It does not seem correct behaviour. It is as bad as two children going at each other with axes, instead of playing decently."

Haldor said, "Talking of playing, there are plenty of old bones lying about on the floor here. If we took the ends off them we could pass the time by playing knuckle-bones. What do you say?"

Harald said, "Yes, we may as well put our hands to some use. At least we shall have this last game to remember."

So until the daylight passed and dusk came down the three men forgot for a while what awaited them. Since they had nothing of value to gamble with, they put their dreams into pawn and won or lost them as the knuckle-bones rose and fell.

Wulf lost his sword to Harald who in turn lost that, and his crown and throne in Norway, to Haldor.

"Fools for luck," said Wulf, pretending to be put out. Then they all laughed wildly, to think how lucky they were in all truth.

Byzantines passing the tower outside in the street heard this strange laughter, tapped their foreheads, shivered and hurried on, as though they were running from ghosts.

39 · Euphemia

The vikings slept little that night. It was as though they could not bear to close their eyes; as though they wished to see everything, even the darkness.

Then, about two hours before dawn, as they lay on their backs in the dust staring up at the circle of sky with the silver stars in it, Harald saw something come whipping over the wall at the top of the tower.

He whispered to the others, who were wide awake, "Do not move yet, brothers, but I think that this is a rope-ladder, and that the Bulgars have come for us. If so, they are early, and I do not approve of losing two hours of life before they carry out the judgement."

Haldor whispered back, "Olaf could not have been listening after all, Harald. Well, that is a risk one must always take with busy Saints. But I tell you one thing, when they come down this ladder I shall not let them take me with them like a meek bullock. I shall leave at least one of them in this prison for the rats to feast on."

Wulf nodded and said, "Aye, that was in my mind too. It is

high time that these rude fellows learned that they must pay something for their entertainment."

Harald said, "I do not know why we did not consider this before. I vote that we each take one, before they can set their feet steadily on the ground, and then we shall go feeling more contented. Besides there is always the chance that if we are able to do enough damage to them, the others will lose their patience and put a quick end to us. I would rather have that than go into the Hippodrome."

Haldor said, "Let us set the price really high, brothers, and see if we can deal with two each as they come down. Now that would give a bit of interest to the game."

So they rolled into the shadow of the wall and waited; but no one came down the rope-ladder. And after a while they heard a woman's voice call softly, "Harald, Harald, hurry or it will be dawn."

Then they went up the swaying ladder carefully and looked out over the top of the tower, and below them in the deserted street stood Maria's lady-in-waiting, Euphemia, wrapped in a grey cloak and looking very frightened. She had a small boy with her who was holding three cloaks and was shivering in the cold breeze of morning that blew off the sea.

And when she saw their heads appear over the high parapet, she called up, "Make haste. Draw the ladder up after you and let it fall down on this side. Then you can come down safely. My brother here will unhook it and hide it somewhere. You can trust him."

Harald said, "Trust him! Why, if I had my way he would be emperor of Byzantium. I trust him that much, lady."

They came down the ladder like ghosts on the wind. And in the street Harald said, "Who sent you, Euphemia? This is the kindest thing that has happened to me in my whole life."

The girl said, "Maria Anastasia sent me. She is a prisoner in her own room in the palace, but she got word to me to do this.

She said that in the night your brother Olaf came to her as a dream and said, 'Now then, woman, less of this moping and wetting the pillow through with tears. They never helped anyone. Be about it and send a ladder to my brother.' It did not sound like a proper Byzantine Saint talking, she thought, but she did what he said, all the same."

Harald said, "She did right. You must never question a Saint, Euphemia. Especially northern Saints. They are brisk fellows and stand on no ceremony. But they get things done."

Wulf said starkly, "Aye, and so must we, brother. So let us be about it, too."

40 · Polota-svarv

The three men ran as swift as wolves away from the squat tower. They had forgotten their hunger and weariness now and in its place there were other feelings to occupy them. As he loped along the narrow streets in the dawn light, Harald was muttering, "Brother Olaf, Brother Olaf, I will light a hundred candles for you in Novgorod."

Wulf stopped once in the middle of the street and looking to the young sun, his arms outstretched, chanted:

> "*In the shed a sheep,*
> *In the byre a bull;*
> *But in the hand a haft!*"

Haldor glanced back and shouted over his shoulder, "Keep running, Icelander. There will be time for poems later."

And so they came to the Via Dolorosa where the narrow cobbled streets ended and the broad avenues began. They took no account of this for there were few folk about so early in the morning. A group of fishermen making their way down to the water with nets slung over their backs saw them but only shook their heads and shrugged. Varangers were always doing strange things and no man whose head sat well on his shoulders tried to stop them.

The flat front of the palace loomed high above the runners now with the dawn sun glinting on its white stone and turning it to honey. It looked down on them blindly with its shutters closed and its striped awnings drawn.

Harald said, "Take care, brothers. Come behind these laurels. The Bulgars are on duty this turn."

Then they reached the alley behind the palace where their own quarters were. And as they passed the barred window that lay down at the level of their feet, they heard many voices, shouting angrily. Wulf said with a grim smile, "Our shipmates are up early. Something must have kept them awake."

The guard on the door, a tall youth from Lund, almost fell down with surprise when Harald pushed past him. "Odin!" he said. "We had given you up! We were just going to take vengeance for you."

Wulf gave him a push which sent his axe clattering and said, "You Norwegians leave it long enough. We could have been white bones before your beef-wits got to work."

But Harald was already in the long dim room, the Varangers crowding round him, slapping his back and shaking his great hand. For a while it was all so noisy that no man could hear himself speak. Then Eystein stood on an ale-tub and shouted, "Silence, lads! We have them back now, so no more talk. Let Harald speak; he has something to say."

Still breathing hard from his running, Harald said, "It has long been in my mind to leave this place, my friends. A man can have too much of the sun, it makes him lazy. Let us say farewell to Miklagard and see what cooks in the Russian pots."

He ran his light eyes over the crowd as they waved their hands and shouted. There were eighty of the best Varangers in that cellar, and most of them armed.

To Eystein he called out, "They took my gear from me when I was arrested, brother. Have you an axe and a shirt to fit me?"

Eystein jumped off his barrel and came with a bundle in his arms. "These are your things, Harald," he said. "Someone flung them down the steps last night and ran away. That was when we thought you must be stark and cold."

As Harald struggled into his hauberk, he said, "A fine thing to wait all night making up your mind."

Eystein shook his head. "You know we can decide nothing without you, lad," he said. "But now you are back we can do everything!"

Harald tightened his belt-buckle carefully and said in a great voice, "Very well, little wolves, then the first thing to do is to claim your booty from the palace while I go about other small tasks."

But Haldor, bleak-faced as a pine, said, "Harald, that is not the law. Varangers may only strip the palace when the emperor has died. That is the ancient custom." He smiled then strangely.

Harald turned on him the gaze of an iceberg before he answered. "You will not break the law, friend. You attend to the foraging, the Polota-svarv, and I will see that the other part of it is arranged."

Then he led the way up the stone steps into the broad corridors where the long silk hangings swung lazily as the Varangers swept past them.

Wulf said as he ran, "I have always had a yearning for an ikon—one with reds and blues and gold on it."

Haldor said, "There is a silver cup in the chapel, with red rubies round the lip. I have often looked at it during Mass. That cup would buy a steading in Sandgill and perhaps three smacks to go fishing in, when the hay-harvest was poor."

Other men said other things; but each had his heart on something. Eystein said, "This Constantine Monomachus has a golden staff, Harald. At my age a man should look to his future. If you see it lying about will you bring it for me?"

Harald nodded but did not answer with words.

And now they were in the central courtyard where the water spouted out of bronze lions' mouths and tall palm trees ringed the fountain like golden pillars. A few Chamberlains in their high crowns were moving about here and there but when they saw the Northmen, they gathered their robes about them and stood aside to let the soldiers pass. No one thought it his affair to raise the alarm.

And so when the Varangers were near the great chapel, Harald halted them and called out, "Be about it, fellows, and join me in the Lion-court when I blow my horn. Do not forget, bring no more than you can carry, running. Doubtless there will be some running to do."

Then he swung away from them along a dusky passageway that was tented with fine red samite hangings. No Varanger followed him there, even in the plunder-fury, for this was a private part of the palace where mostly the women had their lodgings. As Harald came to the first gilded door he paused and drew the heavy curtain aside a little. The empress Zoë was lying on her low divan with the eagles'-claw feet, sprawled in her gauze gown like a great she-cat. Harald looked at the gold on her arms and the many strands of pearl about her wrinkled neck. For a moment a strange smile twisted his golden-bearded lips; then he shrugged his shoulders and went on. "I have never seen an empress sleeping before," he thought. "How helpless they are. As helpless as common folk." But his smile stopped at the next door. Halting only to glance at the long axe in his hand, he ripped open the velvet curtain and ran inside.

While he was away no sound disturbed the corridor; not as

much as a kitten mewing. And when he came back he had the emperor's gold staff in his left hand. "Eystein will be pleased," he said.

The next door he stopped at lay further down the passageway, in a humbler quarter of the great gloomy place. Its curtain was of embroidered linen, not of samite. And here Harald paused a little longer than before, as though less sure of what he was about to do. But in the end he pulled the curtain aside and went in, leaving the axe and the golden staff outside propped by the alabaster wall.

It was only a small room and the curtained bed took up most of its space. Under a great cone of hangings, her black hair spread all over the silk pillows, lay Maria Anastasia. Her dark eyes opened as soon as Harald came through the door but she did not struggle or scream, or do any of the things he had half-expected.

Instead she gazed at him without even moving her head, and said in a faint voice, "You are up early, captain."

Harald stood over her, twisting his golden beard, and then said almost as faintly himself, "Yes, that is because there is much to do, lady. Thank you for giving me the chance to do it."

The princess smiled sadly and said, "Much to do for everyone except me. For me there will only be embroidery and prayers, prayers and embroidery, until I am old and grey."

Harald coughed and looked round the room for Maria's gown.

He said, "All this talk of prayers. I would say you had prayed enough for one night, lady. At any rate, you got a good result. Now, let us be away. You want to leave this place, don't you?"

Maria Anastasia gazed up at him with tears in her eyes. She said, "Now that the moment has come I do not know. When it all seemed impossible, I dreamed every night of escaping with you into the free north. But now that I have the chance, I am afraid. After they took you to the prison last night, the Patriarch came to me and told me most sternly that I was in danger of eternal damnation for offending the caliph and so putting in jeopardy the Church of the Holy Sepulchre in Jerusalem. He said that only by a supreme act of self-denial could I even dream of salvation."

Harald found the gown and handed it to her. He said, "I am not a Patriarch and so I know little about these affairs. But I would say that if you are unhappy here and would be happy elsewhere, then you should take the risk of salvation, whatever that may be."

Maria Anastasia put on her gown and tied the belt. She said, "These things are easy for you, my lord, because you have always pleased yourself in whatever you have done. But my life has been different. I think that I need someone to make up my mind for me."

Harald said, "Very well, then. I will make it up. I will take you away from all these prayers and embroidery and will just throw you into the longship, with my other plunder and perhaps, if I feel like it, I will sell you in Kiev or Polotsk—if you can cook well enough for anyone to want to buy you. Will that do?"

He smiled as he spoke so that she would see he was jesting. Then he turned away to look at a little ikon that hung on the far wall. It was of bright enamels, encrusted with gold and he ran his thick thumb over it lovingly, wondering what it would fetch in Novgorod. Maria came and stood beside him and said, "You may take it, if you like it, Harald. I have never really cared for it; it reminds me too much of the praying and chanting here. Accept it as my passage-money on *Stallion*, captain."

Harald turned towards her and saw that she was smiling and was dressed warmly as for a sea-journey. He said, "I thought you would be screaming for help by now, the way you were talking a moment ago, Maria."

She laughed and said, "No, you have made up my mind for

me, Harald. Just sling me over your shoulder, like the other plunder you spoke of, so that the Chamberlains will be able to report that I was stolen away—and then let us be off."

He did it as gently as he could. Then she reached out and snatched the ikon from the wall. "If you won't take it for yourself," she said, "then I must take it for you."

In the Lion-court the Varangers were already gathered, loaded with all they could lay hands on. When Harald appeared with the princess over his shoulder they shouted and laughed as though they were going on a holiday. Eystein came forward and said, "I see you found the staff for me. Was it any trouble to get it?"

Harald shook his head. "Not for me," he said. "But I suppose there will have to be a period of prayers and mourning, and that will cause old Zoë some trouble. Still, she has her sister to help with the rites, so it will not all fall on one pair of shoulders."

Wulf took him by the arm. "Less talk, more walk," he said sternly. "The Bulgar guard will soon be on the move, and we shall be hampered by all this stuff we are carrying. Come on, a brisk pair of legs will purchase a long life this morning."

41 · The Harbour Chain

They swarmed down the corridors and out to the Via Dolorosa. No one stood in their way; it was as though Byzantium had agreed to let the two shiploads of Varangers go home without hindrance.

Even down at the wharfside all was still and peaceful. Fishermen in their small boats smiled and waved to them, one lot of sailors wishing another lot god-speed.

Haldor said frowning, "I do not like this, brother. A man expects some opposition. He expects a little blood-letting when he gathers plunder. Otherwise it seems to lower the value of the goods."

Harald said, "Save your breath for rowing, Icelander. There may be blood enough to shed before we get clear of Miklagard."

Maria said, across his broad shoulder, "If it comes to that, I shall be sorry I helped you to escape."

Harald said gruffly, "You can always shut your eyes. Now be silent for we are busy men, lady."

He did not like being reminded too often of any debt he owed.

So running they came to the imperial wharf where the galleys and longships were moored. At first they thought there might be some fighting to do, for each longship already had some men aboard, armed with swords and spears. Then Wulf looked at them more closely and said, "They are the men from Hedeby come to join us. We are lucky today and no mistake."

So at last they were in *Stallion* and *War Hawk*, with their plunder stacked hurriedly between the sea-chests. As men slashed the anchor ropes away, Harald almost flung the princess on to a heap of straw in the aftercabin, then turned and cupped his hands to call to the men. "Take place, take place!" he shouted. "Steerboards, set course! Rowers, bend your backs!"

Then the two longships plunged clear of the other craft across the blue water and away from the white quayside.

Now Maria sat up and clasped her hands like a small girl going off on an exciting holiday. Wulf turned and smiled wryly at Haldor. "She may laugh on the other side of her face when she feels how the wind can nip, going up the Dnieper," he said.

Haldor gave his version of a grin and said gently, "Whichever side of her face she smiles on, it will be a pretty smile. I am pleased she is coming with us, brother. I feel that she is my sister now, and one of my life's tasks will be to find a husband worthy of her."

Wulf glanced at him a little sharply, then said in a low voice, "That should cause you no trouble, comrade. I think she has made her own choice already, without your aid."

Then all at once Harald began to roar like a penned bull. "Take care, take care! These sly Greeks have drawn the chain across the harbour mouth."

Eystein Baardson called back from *War Hawk,* "If we halt they will shoot us full of arrows from the shore. Can we ram the chain, brother?"

For a moment Harald's face was as blank as a stone. Then suddenly his frowning stopped and he shouted, "We are in the hand of God, brother. Follow *Stallion* and do as we do. With luck we might still sniff the north wind again."

Fifty oar-strokes away lay the great chain, hitched from barge to barge across the Horn. It was rusted and weed-grown but still stout enough to smash the biggest craft that ran against it. Here and there, between the lighters from which it was suspended, it hung down almost to water-level, in great rusty arcs because of its weight. And it was towards one such arc that Harald steered *Stallion.*

Then calling out loudly so that all should hear his voice, he said, "When I give the sign, let every man run aft with all the plunder he can lift. That might raise the prow above the chain. And when I give the next sign, run forward to get the stern across. That way we might yet leap the fence they have put in our way."

Maria called out pleasantly, "What am I to do, captain? Everyone else has his task."

But Harald did not hear her for now the great chain was coming towards them as fast as a galloping horse.

And when it was only eight paces away, Harald raised his

right hand and yelled, "Now! Back! Back!" And the Varangers raced like men running from a barn fire, their heavy plunder in their arms. *Stallion's* curved prow rose dripping in the morning sun and for a moment seemed about to soar into the sky like a sea-bird. Harald clung to the gunwales, his arms almost wrenched from their sockets, his brow streaming with sweat. Maria Anastasia was flung backwards like a doll, until Wulf put out his foot and held her against the mast-stepping to stop her from going overboard.

Then as *Stallion* straddled the chain, and the oak keel crunched and splintered with the force of the impact, Harald cried out again, "Now forward, men, forward! Run like the wind forward!"

Then the rovers rushed forward, some of them sprawling like drunken men as the longship balanced dangerously for an instant before plunging clear on the farther side of the rusting chain and out into the open sea.

Then they all began to shout and laugh like madmen; until Harald, looking over his shoulder, cried out, "Oh no! Oh no! *War Hawk* has broken her back! See, she is turning turtle! Oh no!"

Four ships' lengths away, on the far side of the chain, *War Hawk* wallowed over heavily, the sea sucking round her, her long mast slapping hard down into the channel like a great sword. The rovers on *Stallion* stared in horror to see the slimy blackened underside of the ship slide upwards, trapping all within it like a bird-snare. Harald gripped the gunwales till his bones showed white. His legs trembled with fear at this sight. He said under his breath, "The water has got them. The sea is devouring them." But he made no move to do anything. He was like a man in a dream that could not be shaken off.

Wulf cried out, "They are lost. Their iron shirts will drag them down, even those who can swim—and few of them can."

Then suddenly Helge who had been leaning beside Haldor

gave a high shout and ran to the side. Harald put out a hand, but was left only with the torn sleeve of the young man's shirt as he plunged overboard.

Helge struck out and got under the chain, and then to the side of *War Hawk*. As the others pulled away on the oars, Harald saw the youth holding up Eystein for a while, trying to get back to the nearest chain-barge. But all at once he flung back his head, seeming to shout out, then went under and Eystein with him.

The tears streamed down Harald's face. He cried, "Pull, pull. They are beyond us, we shall all die if we go back for them."

Only then did Wulf remember that he still had his foot on Maria Anastasia, holding her firmly against the mast-stepping. He took it away but had no words to say to her.

She lay for a long while after that without moving. And then she rose slowly as *Stallion* drew well into the Bosphorus, the towers of Pera-Galata to larboard and those of Chrysopolis to steerboard, and made her way to the after-cabin where she was to have her quarters.

No one dared go to Harald to ask for sailing orders. With Eystein and Helge lost so suddenly, he was like a man who had suffered the punishment of the Hippodrome, wide-eyed and staring with numbness before the true pain came on him and set him howling.

42 · The Parting of the Ways

Three days up through the Black Sea and heading for night-landing at Mesembria, Haldor came to Harald and said, "There is no sense in this. Grief is grief, but if you go on like this you will be useless to yourself and to us. Already the men are losing heart, watching you. Eat something, drink something, and get the strength back to your limbs. What happened was God's will. Who are you, to take all the burden of blame on yourself?"

Harald turned and gazed at him with pale blank eyes, then said in a hoarse voice, "All the years we have been away I have felt every blow which struck a man of mine. Can you, with your wise words, cure me of this now?"

Haldor sat beside him under the forward gunwale and said, "Look, brother, while you live, we live. But if you pine to death because of *War Hawk*, we shall finish out here in the steppelands, among the yellow-faced Patzinaks. We shall never reach home again. Without you, we are already dead men, brother."

Harald considered a while then said, "Haldor, I feel old beyond my years. I feel that I can no longer be held to account for these men. Once it was a glory to me, to be a leader of Varangers. But now I hardly dare set one foot before the other, I am so weary of making decisions."

Wulf came up then and said, "This happens to all great captains who have drained themselves dry of courage for the sake of their men. It is not unusual. Even the greatest of warmen, the Caesar Julius, suffered in his tent before a battle, wondering if he was still worthy."

Harald smiled within himself then said, "Sometimes I think of poor Maniakes. He must have felt like this when he ran away from me to Sicily. If I could meet him again now, in his place of exile, I would take him by the hand and tell him that the long quarrel was over, that the vengeance was taken, one way or another."

When they heard him talking like this, Wulf and Haldor shook their heads and left him. But Maria Anastasia saw all this from her after-cabin and she felt certain in her heart that she could succeed where the rough-speaking vikings had failed. So she went to Harald, walking very softly and daintily, and sat down beside him on the boards.

He was long in noticing that she was there, and then he only said, "Soon we shall be running in the teeth of the north wind. You will be wise to put on furs then."

The princess smiled and took his hard hand. "Harald," she said, "you may be well enough in the thick of a battle, but you are as helpless as a child when there is no fighting to do. You need someone to care for you and to look after you."

He stared at her, then drew his hand away slowly. Maria Anastasia watched it go, then frowned with annoyance and said, "As time goes on you will learn more courtly manners. You will learn how a king must behave."

Harald passed his hand across his lined brow and said, "Who will teach me, woman?"

He spoke as though he did not wish to know the answer, but Maria said quite briskly, "Why, I will. You will see that there are some things I can do for you as time goes on. When we are in the north I will show the folk what it is like to be a Greek. And they will come to do what I teach them to do. They will be glad to follow a civilized example, you will see."

Harald said softly, "If you left me now, I think I could go to sleep, I am so tired."

But Maria Anastasia would not be put off in this way. She smoothed his ruffled hair and said, "You see, Varanger, a new life could open out for you now, with me beside you. Together we could teach the barbarians in the northlands what a king and queen should be like. Why, Byzantium could reach as far to the north as Oslo, or even farther."

Now when she said this Harald gave a great shudder as though she had suddenly drenched him with cold water, and he said like a man coming out of a dream, "I am betrothed to Elizabeth, daughter of King Jaroslav. With the treasure I have sent home from Crete, we shall be married and soon she will sit beside me on the throne in Norway. That is the pattern of my life from now on."

Now it was Maria's turn to shudder. But she would not leave her dream so easily. Taking him by the sleeve and dragging at it, she said, "Listen, Varanger. How dare you say that to me? How dare you even mention another woman's name to me? I am a Greek. I am of the royal house of Argyra. Is that nothing to you?"

Harald smiled sadly and nodded. "Aye," he said, "it is a great deal. Your Aunt Zoë was of that same family."

Suddenly Maria Anastasia rose on the deck and stamped her foot. She said, "I have not come so far from my home to be insulted by a Norse hireling. I have not thrown away all my inheritance to be treated like a servant, and to have the name of some peasant king's brat thrust down my throat. Elizabeth! Elizabeth! Who is this Elizabeth that she must be set above me? Did this precious Elizabeth save your life when you were in the tower prison? Did she send a woman to fetch you out on a rope-ladder? Did she do for you a quarter of what I have done?" She had never spoken so fiercely before, in all her life.

Then for the first time since the harbour chain, Harald stood up as tall as he had ever been, or even taller, and his hard brown face was furrowed in a smile that was awful to see. Even Maria Anastasia backed away from him then, but he took no step towards her to hurt her.

Instead, he said very gently, in a tone that few men had ever heard from his lips before or would hear after, "You remind me that I owe you my life, lady. I shall not remind you of anything you might owe me, because I am sure that among Greeks such a reminder would be considered ill-mannered in a man. You remind me also that you have left a royal palace to come with me to the rude northland."

Then Maria went towards him with her hands out, but he

put them aside and said, "All my life I have been at pains to pay my debts, lady. I am no horse-coper, no market-cheat, no pickpurse at a Fair. I am soon to be the king in Norway, and even in England perhaps. And that is no peasant king, lady."

Now Maria Anastasia saw how things were going and she broke in and said, "Yes, yes, Harald, and you will be a very great king, I am sure of that."

He answered, "Yes, by God's grace and with Saint Olaf's guidance, I might gain some honour. I might grow a little even yet."

Then he half-turned from her and said quite humbly, "But I shall never grow another inch if I am to be reminded for the rest of my days that I owe my very existence to a young woman who threw a rope-ladder over a wall for me to climb up. I shall be a prisoner still, where no ladder would save me."

So he walked the length of the ship with Maria trailing after him, wringing her hands, and he said aloud to Wulf and Haldor, "We shall not put in at Mesembria this evening. But if we stand off shore there and light flares they will send out a rowing boat to us with supplies."

Haldor nodded. "Aye, they will do that, brother," he said.

"Then," answered Harald, "we will pay them well to row this lady with them into port. She shall take with her the ikon I stole from her room and as much treasure as she can carry, to pay her fare back to the royal palace of Byzantium that she yearns after so much already."

Maria Anastasia now burst into tears and fell at his feet on the deck. He looked down at her for a while, then bent and raised her very gently. He said, "Please do not weep, lady. I do not wish my last memory of a Greek princess to be one of weeping. I would rather remember you as the little girl in black who laughed when she rode on my back through the corridors."

Then Maria Anastasia began to cry louder than ever. But

Harald was not there to hear her. He had gone away to the after-cabin and had shut the door and bolted it.

Now he was on his knees in the darkness, giving thanks to God and to Saint Olaf for a safe deliverance from Miklagard.

He did not even come out to see them put Maria Anastasia, still weeping, into the little boat that would take her into Mesembria. Which was just as well, since he had enough memories of sadness to last him a lifetime already. Now he would look forward only to glory.

10